THE GREATEST MARIAN PRAYERS

Visit our web site at
WWW.ALBAHOUSE.ORG

The Greatest Marian Prayers

Their History, Meaning, and Usage

ANTHONY M. BUONO

ALBA·HOUSE   NEW·YORK

SOCIETY OF ST. PAUL, 2187 VICTORY BLVD., STATEN ISLAND, NEW YORK 10314

ST PAULS

Library of Congress Cataloging-in-Publication Data

Buono, Anthony M.
   The greatest Marian prayers: their history, meaning and
usage / Anthony M. Buono.
        p.   cm.
   ISBN 0-8189-0861-0
   1. Mary, Blessed Virgin, Saint — Prayer-books and devotions —
History and criticism.   2. Mary, Blessed Virgin, Saint. Prayer-books
and devotions — English.   I. Title.
BX2160.2.B86   1999
242'.74 — dc21   99-22492
                                                      CIP

Produced and designed in the United States of America by the
Fathers and Brothers of the Society of St. Paul,
2187 Victory Boulevard, Staten Island, New York 10314-6603,
as part of their communications apostolate.

ISBN: 0-8189-0861-0

Printing Information:

Current Printing - first digit   1   2   3   4   5   6   7   8   9   10

Year of Current Printing - first year shown

1999   2000   2001   2002   2003   2004   2005   2006   2007   2008

Acknowledgments

Brief quotations, including the "Litany of the Blessed Virgin Mary," are reproduced from *The Collection of Masses of the Blessed Virgin Mary,* © 1987, 1989 by International Committee on English in the Liturgy. All rights reserved.

A few prayers are reproduced from the *Enchiridion of Indulgences,* © 1969 by Catholic Book Publishing Co. All rights reserved.

Table of Contents

Introduction

$\mathcal{P}$raying to the Blessed Virgin Mary is our Christian heritage. From the beginning Christians have praised Mary as the Mother of God and prayed to her both in the Liturgy and in private devotion. She is "the glory of [the heavenly] Jerusalem,... the surpassing joy of [the new] Israel,... the splendid boast of our [Christian] people" (Judith 15:9).

The theological basis for Marian prayer was set down by Pope Paul VI in his magnificent 1974 Apostolic Exhortation on *Devotion to the Blessed Virgin Mary (Marialis Cultus)*:

"The Church's norm of faith requires that her norm of prayer should everywhere blossom forth with regard to the Mother of Christ. Such devotion to the Blessed Virgin is firmly rooted in the revealed Word and has solid dogmatic foundations.

"It is based on the singular dignity of Mary, Mother of the Son of God, and therefore beloved Daughter of the Father and Temple of the Holy Spirit — Mary, who, because of this extraordinary grace, is far greater than any other creature on earth or in heaven" (no. 56).

The Bishops of the United States explained the meaning of Marian prayer in their splendid 1973 Pastoral Letter *Behold Your Mother*:

"When Mary is honored, her Son is duly acknowledged, loved, and glorified, and his commandments are observed. To venerate Mary correctly means to acknowledge her Son, for she is the Mother of God. To love her means to love Jesus, for she is always the Mother of Jesus.

"To pray to our Lady means not to substitute her for Christ, but to glorify her Son who desires us to have loving confidence in his Saints, especially in his Mother. To imitate the 'faithful Virgin' means to keep her Son's commandments" (no. 82).

MARY IN THE PRAYER OF THE CHURCH

The Word of God tells us that Mary was present with the disciples in prayer at the birth of the Church when the Holy Spirit descended upon the disciples in the Upper Room (cf. Acts 1:14). Therefore, the Church has always made place for Mary in the Liturgy, which is the public prayer of the Body of Christ.

First, the Church *prays to God with Mary.* She takes cognizance of Mary receiving the Word of God and putting it into practice or repeats Mary's great canticle of thanksgiving, the *Magnificat.* She also identifies herself with Mary in the offering of Christ's sacrifice on the Cross or has recourse (at least indirectly) to Mary's intercession in heaven.

Second, the Church *prays to God in honor of Mary.* She "celebrates" the Virgin Mary by praising God for the participation of the Mother of Jesus in the major events of her Son's life. The Church also renders praise to God for the special graces that prepared the Virgin Mary for her mission and for the rewards heaped upon her in body and soul as well as for a number of events in the life of the People of God where Mary's action was particularly evident. Each time also provides the Church with an opportunity to have recourse to the intercession of the Mother of the Church so that her children might follow her example or enjoy her protection.

Third, the Church *prays to Mary*. She speaks directly not to God but to Mary herself — to praise her, to congratulate her in words of the Gospel, and to directly beg for her intercession with her Divine Son and the Blessed Trinity.

However, it is most important to remember that in none of these forms is the prayer to Mary regarded by the Church as an end in itself. It remains completely suitable to serve the worship owed to the true God alone. The Father receives honor and praise for the wisdom of his purposes revealed to Mary. Through the honor paid to his Mother, the Son is better known and loved. And the action of the Holy Spirit in Mary and the Church also is extolled and proclaimed.

In other words, Mary's mediation is not additional to that of Christ, since Mary and Christ are but one in the mystery of his Mystical Body. She brings to those who pray to her the motherly aid of her own prayer, which merges with the supreme prayer of Christ the one Mediator.

MARY IN THE PRAYER OF CHRISTIANS

Thus, Christians from the very beginning have offered prayers to Mary, that is, called upon her, especially in times of adversity — trials, heresies, persecutions, and wars. The reason is not hard to fathom and was spelled out by Pope Leo XIII:

"It has always been the habit of Catholics in danger and in arduous times to fly for refuge to Mary and to seek peace in her maternal goodness, which shows that the Catholic Church has always, and with justice, put all her hope and trust in the Mother of God. She who is associated with her Son in the work of the salvation of the human race has favor and power with him greater than any other human or angelic creature has ever obtained or can obtain.

"And, as it is her greatest pleasure to grant her help and comfort to those who seek her, it cannot be doubted that she will deign, even anxiously, to receive the aspirations of the Universal Church" (Encyclical *Supremi Apostolatus* ["The Supreme Apostolic Office"], September 1, 1883).

The great Doctor of the Church St. Bernard of Clairvaux summed it up even better in this classic way:

> "In danger, anguish, or doubt,
> think of Mary and call upon her.
> Let the name of Mary
> never be far from your lips or heart.
> And to obtain the fruit of her prayers,
> do not forget the example of her life.
> Following Mary,
> you will never lose your way.
> Praying to her,
> you will never sink into despair.
> Contemplating Mary,
> you will never go wrong.
> With Mary's support,
> you will never fall.
> Beneath her protection,
> you will never fear.
> Under her guidance,
> you will never grow weary.
> And with her help,
> you will reach your heavenly goal."

This emphasis of the Church on recourse to Mary on the part of all may account for the fact that the principal Marian prayers are generally by unknown authors. They spring up spontaneously like the various flowers at each season and bear witness to the devotion of all the subsequent Christian centuries.

PRIMITIVE APPEALS TO MARY'S HELP

Right in the first generation of Christians we see the singular honor and devotion heaped upon Mary. The Angel of the Incarnation greets her with the utmost respect as "full of grace" (Luke 1:28), and her cousin Elizabeth does likewise with the words "Mother of my Lord" (Luke 1:43).

The early Church bears witness that the Virgin Mary bears great importance for Christian piety. For example, in the profession of faith she proclaims Christ as Son of God "born of the Virgin Mary" (a second-century formula of the baptismal creed contained in the various apocryphal works of the New Testament, e.g., the *Protevangelium of James*, which is also known as the "Gospel of Mary").

The Church bears similar witness in the Roman funeral monuments of the second-third centuries, e.g., the frescoes in the Priscillian cemetery that show the Prophet Isaiah pointing to the Mother of God seated with the Child Jesus in her arms.

Thirdly, in the *Apostolic Tradition* of Hippolytus, which greatly influenced the Eastern Liturgies, the Church presents the primitive theme of the Virgin in the first part of the Eucharistic Prayer itself: "Sent from heaven into the bosom of the Virgin, conceived in her womb, he was made flesh and manifested himself as [God's] Son, born from the Spirit and from the Virgin."

Mary is thus given a place in the Church's teaching because of her integral connection with the Incarnation of the Son of God. A bit later, the Virgin's association with her Son in the economy of salvation will gain a place for her with him in the Church's thanksgiving. She will be named before the Apostles in the *Communicantes* (Commemoration of the Saints) of the Roman Canon (i.e., Eucharistic Prayer I) or after the Prophets in the chronological listing of the Eastern Anaphora. Hence, Mary is placed on the highest level of the heavenly Church and becomes the first purely human being whose memorial the earthly Church (represented by the Eucharistic Assembly) demands to be celebrated.

The third century brings to the fore the first known prayer to the Virgin Mother of God, the *Sub Tuum*. It calls for her help in trials and sin, while strongly highlighting Mary's Divine Motherhood, virginity, holiness, and powerful intercession in time of adversity.

The fourth century gives us an illustration of the praying Madonna at the cemetery on the Nomentanian Way, i.e., one who intercedes.

The same period presents the patristic *Prayer to the Mother of God*: "Hope of all Christians; pacifier of the Divine wrath; after God, sole refuge, light, strength, riches, glory of all who come to you; the one who assists her devotees in all their contingencies of soul and body; the one whose intercession with God is all-powerful and is put at the disposal of sinners."

FROM THE FIFTH TO THE ELEVENTH CENTURIES

The fifth century sees the arrival of the *Akathist Hymn* (or *Prayer*) with its rich series of terms attesting to Mary's powerful help. And the sixth-seventh centuries manifest the introduction of the first part of the *Hail Mary* into the Mass of the Annunciation.

The sixth-century *Antiphonary* of St. Gregory the Great sets forth texts stemming from the Greek tradition, including the Antiphon: "Rejoice, O Virgin Mary; you have vanquished all heresies in the whole world," which is attributed to the Roman Victor the Blind. Related to this is the Antiphon that has become part of every Office of our Lady: "Make me worthy of praising you, O holy Virgin; grant me strength against your enemies."

The seventh century introduces a hymn (erroneously attributed to St. Ambrose) that invites prayer to the Blessed Virgin: "Therefore, let us pray, O people, to the Virgin Mother of God that she may obtain for us peace and freedom."

At the same time, a sermon on Mary's birth contains the Antiphon that will be repeated in the Office of the Blessed Virgin and at the *Benedictus* of the Marian Office for Saturday: "Holy Mary, succor the miserable, help the weak, comfort the weeping; pray for the people, intervene for the clergy, and intercede for the devoted feminine sex."

That same seventh century provides us with the first invocations of the Litany of Mary including the simple supplication "Holy Mary, pray for us" as well as the first prayers addressed to Mary by St. Ildephonsus of Toledo, which then become part of the Mozarabic liturgical books.

The ninth century sees the liturgical reformer Alcuin of York compile a *Sacramentary* for private devotion that contains two Votive Masses of the Blessed Virgin that form a prelude to the Office of Mary with prayers to Mary.

The tenth century manifests the continuation of prayers to the Virgin expressed in litanaic invocations and hymns. One example is the prayer of Odo of Cluny who is accustomed to call the Blessed Virgin "Mother of Mercy." This phrase then becomes part of the Litany of Loreto and ends up in the primitive text of the *Salve Regina Misericordiae*, "Hail Queen of Mercy."

The eleventh century brings into play beautiful prayers such as the *Salve Regina* ("Hail, Holy Queen") and the *Alma Redemptoris Mater* ("Mother Benign of Our Redeeming Lord"), which call upon Mary's powerful help.

FROM THE TWELFTH TO THE SIXTEENTH CENTURIES

The twelfth century brings forth the Antiphon *Ave Regina Caelorum* ("Hail, O Queen of Heaven"), which celebrates the glory of the Queen of Heaven, who gave birth to Christ, the Light of the World.

The fourteenth century sees the composition of the *Stabat Mater* ("At the Cross Her Station Keeping"), the great heart-shattering hymn of the sufferings of compassion endured by the Blessed Virgin at the foot of the Cross. At the same time, the *Angelus* ("The Angel of the Lord Declared unto Mary") commemorates the great moment of the Incarnation when, through Mary's "Yes," the Son of God became Man in her womb.

The fifteenth century brings to light the final version of the *Litany of Loreto*, the Litany of the Mother of Christ and Virgin for the world, a Helper for us and a Queen for the Angels. At the same time, it sets forth the final form of the *Rosary*. In it we ask the Blessed Virgin to unite our poor sorrows and our poor victories with her own and immerse them in the joys, sorrows, and victories of her Son. In this way, our sorrows may not be bitter, and our victories may always be magnanimous. The same century sees the appearance of the moving popular prayer of the *Memorare* ("Remember...").

The sixteenth century brings the final version of the *Hail Mary*. The first part, which is taken from the Gospel, was most likely used as a prayer from the very first century and (as already mentioned) eventually appeared in an Entrance Antiphon of the Mass around the sixth century. Then during the twelfth century it began to spread among the faithful.

The second part ("Holy Mary...") consisting of elements that preexisted in a separated state, was put together beginning with the fifteenth century and came into use among the faithful a little after 1500.

The above-mentioned prayers are only a few of the countless ones composed in Mary's honor throughout the centuries. They are, as it were, the *most well known and quasi-official Marian Prayers*, and they have remained in the forefront of prayers to our Lady to the present time.

The following chapters will set forth a short commentary on twelve of these quasi-official prayers to our Lady. It is my hope that knowledge of these Marian prayers will help keep them alive in the hearts, minds, and lives of Catholics today.

As an additional aid, an Appendix reproduces what might be termed *classic unofficial Marian Prayers*. They have been known and used to a lesser extent and deserve to be reproduced in a book of this kind.

THE GREATEST MARIAN PRAYERS

1

The Hail Mary

*I*n a way, the Hail Mary summarizes the whole of the Church's public prayers to Mary. For this Marian prayer was in its *initial form* among the first to be used in the Church and in its *completed form* among the last to be used of those treated — being finally put together in the fifteenth century and finalized in the sixteenth.

The prayer may be divided into two major parts: (1) the Evangelical Salutation (cf. Luke 1:28 and 42) and (2) the Supplication of the Church. The first part was used very early in the Church. A formula of the two scriptural salutations that make up the first part is found in the Eastern Liturgies of St. James of Antioch and St. Mark of Alexandria, which may date from the fifth or even fourth century. It is also part of the Liturgy of the Abyssinian Jacobites and the ritual of St. Severus (538).

In addition, this first part also appears on an Egyptian potsherd of the sixth century with the additional words "Because you have conceived Christ, the Son of God, Redeemer of our souls." The word *Mary* is added in some copies of the Liturgy of St. James, and the words "Mary, Virgin Mother of God" in some Greek churches.

The first appearance of the Salutation in the Western Church occurs as an Offertory Antiphon for the feast of the Annunciation, Ember Wednesday in December, and the Fourth Sunday of Advent.

USE IN THE DIVINE OFFICE

In time, specifically the eleventh century, the Angelic Salutation was incorporated into the Hours of the *Little Office of the Blessed Virgin Mary*, which was added for devotional reasons to the *Divine Office* by numerous religious orders and then adopted by secular clergy and laity. The addition of the word "Jesus" at the end is ascribed to Pope Urban IV (1261-1264).

The first part of the Hail Mary was accustomed to be recited one hundred and fifty times in imitation of the Psalter.

The second part — Supplication of the Church — is thought to have been added because of the Marian invocation in the Litany of the Saints: "Holy Mary, pray for us," introduced toward the end of the seventh century. It was probably inserted because of the idea that greeting and praise to Mary should lead to some type of impetration.

An eleventh century hymn to Mary attributed to Gottschalk of Aachen has Gabriel's words as its first stanza and six remaining stanzas culminating in the words:

> "Come to our aid
> now and at the hour of death,
> and at the end of the world
> acknowledge us as your own."

These words seem to foreshadow the petition in the form known to us. The words "Holy Mary, Mother of God, pray for us sinners" appear in sermons of St. Bernardine of Siena (d. 1444), in Carthusian Breviaries of the sixteenth century, and in synodal decrees of Augsburg and Constance from 1567. The Hail Mary also appeared in some way in Mercedarian, Camaldolese, and Franciscan Breviaries of the sixteenth century.

In 1568, the *Roman Breviary* of Pope Pius V was published with the complete Hail Mary (as it is today) prescribed to be said at the beginning of each canonical Hour. This practice was followed until suppressed by Pius XII in his modified reform of the Breviary on March 23, 1955.

In the new *Liturgy of the Hours* (the revision of the *Roman Breviary*), the Hail Mary is given only as an optional antiphon for the end of Night Prayer. However, it is a fixture on the lips of Catholics in the recitation of the Rosary and the Angelus as well as in untold numbers of other devotions, for example triduums and novenas of all kinds.

> *Hail Mary, full of grace,*
> *the Lord is with you (thee)!* (LUKE 1:28)
> *Blessed are you (art thou) among women,*
> *and blessed is the fruit of your (thy) womb, Jesus.*
> (LUKE 1:42)
>
> *Holy Mary,*
> *Mother of God,*
> *pray for us sinners,*
> *now and at the hour of our death.*

> (Latin Version)
> *Ave Maria, gratia plena,*
> *Dominus tecum!*
> *Benedicta tu in mulieribus*
> *et benedictus fructus ventris tui, Iesus.*
>
> *Sancta Maria,*
> *Mater Dei,*
> *ora pro nobis peccatoribus,*
> *nunc et in hora mortis nostrae.*

THE EVANGELICAL SALUTATION (LUKE 1:28 AND 42)

Hail Mary. Scholars tell us that the first word of the Angel Gabriel was really "Rejoice!" We follow the Vulgate in making it the equivalent of the common greeting in Greek, "Hail." At the same time, we are mindful of the idea of rejoicing by recalling the Messianic joy announced by the Prophets to the "Daughter of Zion," the personification of the Remnant of Israel: "Shout for joy, O Daughter of Zion! Sing joyfully, O Israel.... The Lord, your God, is in your midst, a mighty savior" (cf. Zephaniah 3:14-17; cf. Zechariah 9:9).

The Church adds the name of Mary, whom we are addressing. It reminds us of the sister of Moses who led the singing and thanksgiving at God's great saving deed of the Exodus (cf. Exodus 15:2-21).

Full of grace. The more modern Scripture texts have "highly favored daughter" or "favored one" instead of the classical "full of grace." No matter which is used, the meaning is the same — Mary is the recipient of the Divine favor, that is, of the sanctifying power of God in view of her office of Mother of the Messiah, which the Angel announces to her in verses 31 and 35.

Pope John Paul II, in the encyclical *Mother of the Redeemer* (no. 8), offers a splendid spiritual commentary on this phrase:

"When we read that the messenger addresses Mary as 'full of grace,' the Gospel context, which mingles revelations and ancient promises, enables us to understand that among all the 'spiritual blessings in Christ' this is a special 'blessing.' In the mystery of Christ she is *present* even 'before the creation of the world,' as the one whom the Father 'has chosen' as *Mother* of his Son in the Incarnation. And, what is more, together with the Father, the Son has chosen her, entrusting her eternally to the Spirit of holiness.

"In an entirely special and exceptional way Mary is united to Christ, and similarly she *is eternally loved in this 'beloved Son,'* this Son who is of one being with the Father, in whom is concentrated all the 'glory of grace.' At the same time, she is and remains perfectly open to this 'gift from above' (cf. James 1:17). As the Council teaches, 'Mary stands out among the poor and humble of the Lord, who confidently await and receive salvation from him.'"

The Lord is with you (thee). These words are a reminder that the task entrusted to Mary for the salvation of the world is far beyond all human power. It requires the power of God. So God is with her.

The words recall God's words to Moses when the latter was fearful of the task given him by God: "I will be with you" (Exodus 3:12). They also conjure up the Angel's words to Gideon when the latter was about to receive the mission to save Israel: "The Lord is with you, O champion!" (Judges 6:12).

Blessed are you (art thou) among women. This is a Hebraism for "more blessed are you than all women." In Elizabeth's inspired words, Mary is "blessed" because she will give birth to the Son of God who will bring salvation, and thus she is truly deserving to be called the Mother of God. These words seem to be modeled upon the blessing addressed to Judith (a type of Mary) by the people whom she had just saved from slavery and death: "Blessed are you, daughter, by the Most High God, above all women on earth" (Judith 13:18).

These words of the prayer recall the words that Elizabeth addressed to Mary three verses later (even though they are not part of the Hail Mary): "And blessed is she who believed that there would be a fulfillment of what was spoken to her from the Lord" (Luke 1:45). Once more Pope John Paul II offers a fine analysis:

"These words can be linked with the title 'full of grace' of the Angel's greeting. Both of these texts reveal an essential Mariological content, namely the truth about Mary who has become really present in the mystery of Christ precisely because she 'has believed.' The *fullness of grace* announced by the Angel means the gift of God himself. *Mary's faith*, proclaimed by Elizabeth at the Visitation, indicates *how* the Virgin of Nazareth *responded to this gift*" (*Ibid.*, no. 12).

And blessed is the fruit of your (thy) womb, Jesus. Mary is the woman chosen by God to give birth to the one who was to bring salvation. On Mary and the Child rest the Divine blessing and the praise of human beings. In Jesus the Church recognizes, with Mary, the Blessed One in person.

THE SUPPLICATION OF THE CHURCH

Holy Mary. Mary's holiness is greater than that of all the Angels and Saints combined. She is the Immaculate Conception, "full of grace." In the words of the Second Vatican Council, "From the first instant of her conception she was adorned with the radiance of an entirely unique holiness" (*Constitution on the Church*, no. 56).

Mary was all holy and exempt from sin. For sin always means denial that leads away from God. Mary was never away from God. Like the servant of Psalm 123, she kept her eyes on her Lord to do his will at the least sign of it.

From birth Mary was filled with the Holy Spirit and displayed the theological virtues throughout her life. Her peerless faith enabled her to be in complete accord with her Son's mission and to become his associate in the Redemption. Her indomitable hope kept her going even in the face of Jesus' death on Calvary. And her universal charity embraces all human beings in the boundless love she has for her Son who is her God.

Mother of God. This is a title that expresses the belief of the Church (and those who say the prayer) in the reality of the Incarnation, the Son of God born of Mary for our salvation. Jesus' human nature from the first moment of its existence was congenitally united with the Divine Nature in the Person of the Word. This means that it is as man that he was sole Savior, only Mediator, and the Priest, Prophet, and King beyond compare. And it was Mary's motherly action, under the power of the Holy Spirit, that resulted in this.

Jesus prepared for himself a Mother worthy of himself, a "worthy Mother of God," completely dedicated to her singular vocation: "Redeemed by reason of the merits of her Son and united to him by a close and indissoluble tie, she is endowed with the high office and dignity of the Mother of the Son of God and, in consequence, the beloved daughter of the Father and the temple of the Holy Spirit. Because of this sublime grace she far surpasses all creatures, both in heaven and on earth" (*Ibid.*, no. 53).

Pray for us sinners. These words of the prayer ask Mary to intercede on our behalf, sinners that we all are. They call to mind the words of the tax collector in Christ's parable: "Be merciful to me, a sinner" (Luke 18:13).

By them, we ask for Mary's prayer, which is first of all a prayer of praise and thanksgiving: the *Magnificat*. And she invites all her children to make use of it.

At the same time, it is also an act of supplication for us. Aware of the power of the prayer of the Mother of God, to whom her Son wants to refuse nothing, Christians come to her as mendicants. Hence, every sincere prayer qualifies for presentation by Mary to Jesus. And through Mary, uniting it with her own motherly worship, every sincere prayer can be offered in the expectation of being heard.

Indeed, Mary in heaven is not insensitive to the afflictions of her children on earth. The French theologian Jean Galot has said: "The state of glory enables [Mary] to sympathize with [those afflictions] more completely, since this state opens wide her heart to the dimensions of God's love.

"Ever since her passage to the beyond, our sufferings and our needs reverberate all the more in Mary. Her intercession proceeds from genuine compassion toward us, and the feelings of pity and mercy that we attribute to her are not pure metaphor."

Now and at the hour of our death. The supplication we ask for from Mary is for the present time and especially at the time of our death. It is to aid our passage to our heavenly home. And from the earliest times Catholics have prayed the Hail Mary in whole or in part for this grace — the grace of a happy death.

This is indicated by the practice of saying three Marys for final perseverance. At the same time, there is the well-known invocation to the Holy Family:

"Jesus, Mary, Joseph, I give you my heart and my soul.

"Jesus, Mary, Joseph, assist me in my last agony.

"Jesus, Mary, Joseph, may I breathe forth my soul in peace with you."

THE POWER OF THE PRAYER

The Hail Mary has been endorsed by the Church many times over. It is used in countless devotions, be they liturgical, paraliturgical, or private.

It has been the favorite of many Saints, for example, St. Alphonsus Liguori, who recommended its recitation without reservation.

One of its most fervent adherents was St. Louis Marie Grignion de Montfort. He wrote: "The Angelic Salutation is a most concise summary of all that Catholic theology teaches about the Blessed Virgin. It is divided into two parts, that of praise and that of petition. The first shows all that goes to make up Mary's greatness; and the second, all that we need to ask her for, and all that we may expect to receive through her goodness" (*Secret of the Rosary*, no. 44).

He also cited the wonderful quote of Blessed Alan de la Roche on the power of this prayer:

"Whenever I say Hail Mary, the court of heaven rejoices and earth is lost in wonderment; I despise the world and my heart is filled with the love of God when I say, 'Hail Mary.' All my fears wilt and die and my passions are quelled if I say, 'Hail Mary'; devotion grows within me and sorrow for sin awakens when I say, 'Hail Mary.'

"Hope is made strong in my breast and the dew of consolation falls on my soul more and more because I say, 'Hail Mary.' And my spirit rejoices and sorrow fades away when I say, 'Hail Mary'" (*Ibid.*, no. 55).

We could do no better than to close with the words of St. Louis himself in praise of the power of this wonderful prayer:

"The Hail Mary is the most beautiful of all prayers. It is the perfect compliment the Most High God paid to Mary through his Archangel in order to win her heart.... If you say the Hail Mary properly, this compliment will infallibly earn you Mary's goodwill.

"When the Hail Mary is well said, that is, with attention, devotion, and humility, it is, according to the Saints, the enemy of Satan, putting him to flight; it is... a source of holiness for souls, a joy to the Angels, and a sweet melody for the devout. It is the Canticle of the New Testament, a delight for Mary, and glory for the Blessed Trinity" (*True Devotion to Mary*, nos. 252-253).

2

The Magnificat

A LITURGICAL CANTICLE

*F*rom the third to the fourth century, the Liturgy chanted in the Divine Office the three canticles of the New Testament: the *Benedictus* (be-ne-DIK-tuhs) (Luke 1:68-79), the *Magnificat* (mag-NIF-i-kaht) (Luke 1:46-55), and the *Nunc Dimittis* (nuhnk di-MIT-is) (Luke 2:29-32). The *Magnificat* was used sometimes at the Office of Readings (i.e., Matins) and sometimes at Evening Prayer (i.e., Vespers).

In the East, it was chanted each day at the Office of Readings in the Byzantine Liturgy (with a trope repeated after each verse) and also in the Armenian and Syro-Maronite Liturgies.

In the West, it was part of the Office of Readings in the Gallican Liturgy. In the Roman Rite, it was chanted at the end of Evening Prayer. The *Rule of St. Benedict* (c. 530) is the most ancient witness to this usage of unknown origin. Scholars surmise that the *Magnificat* was originally chanted at the Office of Readings as in the other rites and was assigned to Evening Prayer toward the end of the fifth century. This was after the Council of Ephesus (431) when Marian devotion developed in the West, notably at Rome.

Since it is a canticle of joy and thanksgiving, the *Magnificat* has often been chanted at the conclusion of various Church celebrations. In eighth-century Rome, it was chanted at the end of the baptismal procession that took place each day of Easter Week. In France, until recently it was chanted in many parishes after the Sunday High Mass.

In the *Missal of Paul VI*, the *Magnificat* is used as the Gospel reading for the feasts of the Visitation and the Assumption. And in the new *Collection of Masses of the Blessed Virgin Mary*, it is used in the Gospel of three of the forty-six Masses: No. 3: The Visitation of the Blessed Virgin Mary; No. 39: Holy Mary, Queen and Mother of Mercy, II; and No. 44: The Blessed Virgin Mary, Health of the Sick.

THE *MAGNIFICAT* IN SCRIPTURE

The *Magnificat* is Mary's masterpiece, a prayer that Catholics have loved and used throughout the ages. It is a prayer that preannounces the values of the Beatitudes, alluding to a Kingdom of God that belongs to the poor, the meek, the afflicted, the needy, and to those who show mercy, to the poor, to the peaceful, and to the persecuted.

The text of this prayer is found in chapter one, verses 46-55, of St. Luke's Gospel. After Mary hears and accepts the Angel's announcement that she will be the Mother of the Messiah, the Son of God, she quickly undertakes a three-day journey to visit her cousin Elizabeth who is with child.

Upon seeing Mary, Elizabeth is filled with the Holy Spirit and exclaims: "Blessed are you among women, and blessed is the fruit of your womb.... Blessed is she who has believed that the promise made to her by the Lord will be fulfilled" (Luke 1:42-45). These two "blessings" refer directly to the Annunciation.

When Elizabeth's greeting bears witness to that culminating moment of Christ's Incarnation in her, Mary's faith acquires a new consciousness and a new experience. She responds with the *Magnificat*, whose title comes from the first word of its Latin translation meaning "magnifies" or "proclaims the greatness." It is a canticle wholly permeated by the faith and hope of the People of God of the Old Testament. Not surprisingly, it has become the song of predilection of the People of God in the New Testament.

There are a multitude of translations of this prayer. Even those used in the Liturgy differ. The text used in the Gospel readings is that of the *New American Bible*. The text used in the *Liturgy of the Hours* is that of the International Consultation on English Texts. For our purposes, we will follow the latter.

> *My soul proclaims the greatness of the Lord,*
> *my spirit rejoices in God my Savior.*
>
> *For he has looked with favor on his lowly servant.*
> *From this day all generations will call me blessed:*
> *the Almighty has done great things for me,*
> *and holy is his Name.*
> *He has mercy on those who fear him*
> *in every generation.*
>
> *He has shown the strength of his arm,*
> *He has scattered the proud in their conceit.*
> *He has cast down the mighty from their thrones,*
> *and has lifted up the lowly.*
> *He has filled the hungry with good things,*
> *and the rich he has sent away empty.*
>
> *He has come to the help of his servant Israel*
> *for he has remembered his promise of mercy,*
> *the promise he made to our fathers,*
> *to Abraham and his children for ever.*

REVEALS MARY'S HEART

In addition to heaping on God *joyful praise*, the *Magnificat* reveals Mary's heart: (a) her *humility* as she praises God; (b) her *strength* as she remains God-centered; (c) her *spirit of prayer* as she prays in the spirit of the psalms and prayers of the Old Testament; and (d) her *knowledge of salvation history* as she sets forth salvation themes in summary form.

These themes may be outlined as follows. (a) Salvation is accorded to the *Anawim*, also known as the Poor of the Lord (or Poor of Yahweh) (cf. Zephaniah 3:12), and usually translated as the *lowly*. (b) The salvation to be accomplished by Mary's Son will be another (and greater) Exodus and Return from the Exile. (c) The Suffering Servant of Isaiah (the Poor of the Lord par excellence) will be upheld in remembrance of the promises made to Abraham, the father of God's People, especially the Poor of the Lord.

Mary was the greatest representative of the Poor of the Lord, of those pious Jews from ancient times who believed in the Lord and put their trust in him alone. Theirs was a "poverty of being" not simply one of money. They were the "remnant" of whom the Prophets spoke, who would remain faithful to the Lord and inherit the promises he had made (cf. Isaiah 6:13; 37:31; Micah 4:6-7).

Thus, Mary was at the head of the New Testament community of the Poor of the Lord that included Zechariah, Elizabeth, the Shepherds at the crib, the afflicted, widows, and orphans as opposed to the proud and the self-sufficient who trusted in their own strength with no need of the Lord.

These pious ones did not trust in themselves but in the Lord. They knew that as the Spirit of God worked in the primeval darkness to produce all that exists, so the Lord worked on his "poor" to produce all that is good for them.

It was the Lord who created a *land* for that people by uprooting the inhabitants of Palestine before them. And it was the Lord who gave them the *Law* through Moses. In all these cases, human power would have availed them nothing.

The *Magnificat* is pervaded by references to the Old Testament (the only Scriptures in Mary's day), especially the Psalms, which formed the Prayerbook of the Poor of the Lord. Indeed, we can say that the canticle of Mary is the "Christian Psalm" par excellence.

It may be divided as follows:

(1) Introductory Praise (vv. 46-47)
(2) Strophe One: God's Goodness to Mary (vv. 48-50)
(3) Strophe Two: God's Goodness to His People (vv. 51-53)
(4) Conclusion: Fulfillment of God's Promises (vv. 54-55)

INTRODUCTORY PRAISE (VV. 46-47)

My soul proclaims the greatness of the Lord, my spirit rejoices in God my Savior (vv. 46-47 — cf. I Samuel 2:1; Isaiah 61:1). Mary praises God and rejoices in him as her Savior. She knows that the birth of the Child announced to her will inaugurate God's decisive act of salvation.

The Virgin of Nazareth is overwhelmed by the extraordinary honor God has bestowed on her. For she regards herself as unworthy to be the Mother of the long-awaited Messiah, Son of David and Son of God (cf. Luke 1:32, 35).

What was hidden in the depths of the "obedience of faith" at the Annunciation can now be said to spring forth like a clear and life-giving flame of the spirit. Mary's words are an inspired profession of her faith, in which her response to the revealed Word is expressed with the religious and poetic exultation of all her being toward God.

The sole source of her joy is God her Savior. The exultation she feels is the delight of the Poor of the Lord. It is the delight of the last days, the great longing of joy that at last is fulfilled with the arrival of the Messiah.

Together with them, Mary waits in the name of all Israel and in the name of all creation for the coming redemption.

STROPHE ONE:
GOD'S GOODNESS TO MARY (VV. 48-50)

This strophe gives the reasons for praising God on the part of Mary and the Poor of the Lord.

For he has looked with favor on his lowly servant. From this day all genera-tions will call me blessed. The Almighty has done great things for me, and holy is his Name (vv. 48-49 — cf. I Samuel 1:11; Psalms 71:19; 111:9; 126:2f). Mary indicates that the awesome privilege bestowed on her will lead Christians of all time to call her blessed — although she is a lowly servant of the Lord.

The Church's attitude toward Mary is beautifully sketched in the words of the Intercessions for Morning Prayer of Saturday of Week III in the Latin edition of the *Liturgy of the Hours*: "[From all eternity] God chose Mary to be the Mother of Christ. Therefore, she is above all other creatures both in heaven and on earth."

The Motherhood of the Messiah is the greatest of the "great things" God has done for Mary. It is the last of a long line of great things that God has done, among which was the deliverance of his people from Egypt (cf. Deuteronomy 10:19-22).

He has mercy on those who fear him in every generation (v. 50 — cf. Exodus 20:6; Psalms 85:9; 103:17). Mary extols God's mercy shown to those who fear him — that is, the Poor of the Lord in the his-tory of the People of God of the Old Testament and now of the New. She emphasizes three attributes of God most admired by the Poor — mighty, holy, and merciful!

STROPHE TWO:
GOD'S GOODNESS TO HIS PEOPLE (vv. 51-53)

In this strophe the reasons for praising God are less personally those of Mary and more those of the Poor. By the aorist tense of the verbs used, Mary indicates that the actions of God they express are his normal way of acting, yet they will be intensified through the Child to be born.

He has shown the strength of his arm, he has scattered the proud in their conceit (v. 51 — cf. Job 5:12; Psalms 33:6; 98:1; 138:6; Sirach 10:14; Isaiah 40:10). Mary notes that the Divine power is exercised against the *proud*. Pride affects the spirit, but it flows from a disordered love of self.

For the Israelites, the heart was the seat of desires and thoughts. Thus, this verse does not deal with the enemies of Israel or the Poor but with all who have the sin of pride. Applied to Mary, this means that by making her the Mother of the Messiah through a virginal conception God confounded human pride and the wisdom of the world.

He has cast down the mighty from their thrones, and has lifted up the lowly (v. 52 — cf. Job 5:11; Psalms 75:8; 113:7; Sirach 10:14). This verse transmits a well-known theme in Judaism: abasement of the mighty and elevation of the lowly. Mary gives it a more precise meaning. The Messiah-King, humble Son of the Virgin of Nazareth, will be elevated, take his place as King of the Jews, and substitute his authority for that of the usurpers.

He has filled the hungry with good things, and the rich he has sent away empty (v. 52 — cf. 1 Samuel 2:5; Psalms 34:10f; 107:9; Ezekiel 34:29). Mary sings God's praises for filling the hungry with good things while sending the rich empty away.

This image comes from the court etiquette of the East where only the rich were allowed entry. They offered their presents and received others back. God's way of acting, says Mary, is different.

He is generous to those who ask with humility and deaf to those who think they have the right to demand. The goods Mary speaks about are not material riches but Messianic blessings, as suggested by the entire canticle and especially by the next verse.

One of the marks of the Messianic Kingdom will be the evangelization of the lowly (cf. Isaiah 61:1). Indeed, Mary anticipates her Son's teaching that wealth and power are not real values since they have no standing in God's sight.

CONCLUSION:
FULFILLMENT OF GOD'S PROMISES (VV. 54-55)

He has come to the help of his servant Israel for he has remembered his promise of mercy (v. 54 — cf. Psalm 98:3; Isaiah 41:9; Jeremiah 31:3, 20). Mary begins the conclusion of the canticle by pointing out that the mercy of God has been affirmed in favor of his servant Israel. This intervention on behalf of Israel alludes only secondarily to the distant past, to the benefits accorded the house of Jacob.

It alludes primarily to the event that has just been realized, the conception of the Messiah. God has not forgotten his People despite all the trials they had merited and undergone. He has remembered his promises of old.

The promise he made to our fathers, to Abraham and his children for ever (v. 55 — cf. Genesis 13:15; 22:18; Psalm 132:11; Micah 7:20). Mary specifies what promises are meant. In Micah 7:20 ("you will be faithful to Jacob, propitious to Abraham, as you have promised to our fathers") the Prophet has in view the people issued from Jacob and Abraham. In the *Magnificat*, the meaning is more individual. God's intervention is manifested in favor of Abraham, called with all his race to enjoy the Messianic benefits (cf. John 8:56).

This does not refer only to the People of God of the Old Testament. Abraham was the *father of all believers*. This promise would then have to do with all peoples, who will be blessed in Abraham. Israel was to be the light of the nations (cf. Isaiah 42:6-7); through it the Messianic salvation was to be communicated to all others.

The end of the canticle marks the definitive character of God's new intervention. It will last forever.

MAKING THE *MAGNIFICAT* OUR OWN

In her canticle and in herself, Mary recalls some of the great women of the Old Testament who were liberators of their fellow human beings on earth, defending the justice and glory of God and the love of his people.

Among these were: Miriam, Prophetess and helpmate, who saved Moses from a cruel death and was instrumental in the Exodus; Deborah, Prophetess and Judge, a mother in Israel (cf. Judges 4:4); Judith, the glory of Jerusalem, who walked uprightly before God (cf. Judith 13:20; 15:9); and Esther, wise and beautiful Queen, who saved her people from extermination (cf. Esther 6-8).

The Virgin Mother is constantly present on the journey of faith of the People of God toward the light. Thus, the *Magnificat* that welled up from the depths of Mary's faith ceaselessly reechoes in them down through the centuries — at many moments of both personal and communal devotion.

We should strive to make the *Magnificat* our own by thinking of the deeds God did on our behalf for which we can praise him. All our encounters of life ultimately come from God and have contributed to making us the persons we are.

Repeating, with Mary, the words of the *Magnificat*, we are sustained by the power of God's truth, proclaimed on that occasion with such extraordinary simplicity. At the same time, by means of this truth about God we are enlightened about the different and sometimes tangled paths of our earthly existence.

3

The Sub Tuum

THE OLDEST MARIAN PRAYER

*I*f we were asked to name the oldest prayer to the Blessed Virgin Mary, what would we answer? Most of us would probably say the *Hail Mary* — but we would be wrong.

The complete *Hail Mary* did not come into effect as a prayer until the fifteenth or sixteenth century. Obviously, the words of the first part of this favorite prayer can be traced back to New Testament times. However, they were woven into a prayer only many years afterward, and the second part came into play solely in the Middle Ages.

On the other hand, the Marian prayer that can legitimately be held up as the oldest is a short supplication addressed to Mary known as the *Sub Tuum* (suhb TOO-uhm) from the first two words of its Latin translation. In English it is usually entitled "We Fly to Your Patronage."

> *We fly to your patronage,*
> *O holy Mother of God;*
> *despise not our petitions in our necessities,*

but deliver us always from all dangers,
O glorious and blessed Virgin.

In medieval times, the *Sub Tuum* had been introduced into the liturgical prayer of the Church — forming part of the *Divine Office*, now known as the *Liturgy of the Hours*. For hundreds of years, it has been one of the four Marian anthems to be recited at the conclusion of Night Prayer (formerly known as Compline).

HISTORY OF THE PRAYER

There is good reason to believe that this may be termed a lived prayer — one whose words were fashioned out of pressing need. When it was first used by Christians, the "dangers" mentioned were a harsh reality for those who uttered the words — dangers that spelled fierce persecution and horrible death. For although this deceptively simple prayer was once regarded as dating from the Middle Ages, it really goes back to third-century Egypt.

At that time, Christians were being battered by the persecution of the Roman Emperors Septimius Severus (193-211) and Decius (249-251) and decimated by deportations. Therefore, it was all too natural for such a short spontaneous prayer to rise constantly to their lips. From them, it passed on to other Christians, especially in their worship.

In the Coptic Rite of the third century, for instance, the *Sub Tuum* was part of the liturgical office of Christmas. At the end of that century, Patriarch Theonas of Alexandria built the first real church for local Christians (who prior to that time were accustomed to assemble in homes and cemeteries) and called it the Church of St. Mary Virgin and Mother of God. Thus, it is evident that Alexandrian Christians were already calling Mary the "Mother of God" in the third century — long before St. Athanasius, who was usually credited with coining the phrase.

Indeed, the title "Mother of God" was a traditional one in

Egypt even before the advent of Christianity. It was originally the title given to Isis, mother of the god Horus. The Coptic Christians, quite naturally, bestowed this title on Mary — and they did so even before the Council of Ephesus officially endorsed this exalted title for Mary in 431.

In addition, the great Alexandrian theologian Origen, who lived at the beginning of the third century, set forth the reason why Mary could rightfully be called the Mother of God. And the Greek term for "Mother of God," *Theotokos* — because of its popularity in the Egyptian Church — became a hallowed Marian title.

Thus, the *Sub Tuum* may be regarded as a precious heritage of the Egyptian Church, which tradition tells us was founded by St. Mark the Evangelist. It is just another of the contributions of this Church that aided the formulation of the Christian Faith and also assisted at the birth of the monastic movement.

In 1917, an innocent-looking papyrus leaf originating in Egypt found its way into the John Rylands Library of Manchester, England. This set in motion a series of events that had a great effect on Mariology. By the time the experts completed their painstaking work of examining this three-and-a-half by seven inch papyrus and the ten lines of Greek letters inscribed in capitals on it, the year was 1938 and the term "Mother of God" was proven to have been addressed to Mary a hundred years before previously thought.

FIRST LINE: REFUGE IN MARY

The first line of the prayer (*"We fly to your patronage"*) immediately sets the stage for the ensuing petition. The words it comprises — which could also be translated as "We run to your protection" — eliminate all ambiguity. They take for granted that Mary has the power as well as the will to protect her children.

These first words flow directly from the fact that Mary is our Mother. In the words of St. Alphonsus Liguori: "When Mary's clients call her mother, they are not using empty words. She *is* our Mother — not by flesh, of course, but spiritually; the Mother of our souls, of our salvation."

In addition, the word used for "patronage" or "protection" comes from the Septuagint (the Greek translation of the Old Testament made in the third century B.C.) and is found in the following Bible texts:

Isaiah 49:2: "[The Lord] concealed me in the shadow of his arm."
Isaiah 51:16: "I have... shielded you in shadow of my hand."
Psalm 17:8: "Hide me in the shadow of your wings."

Hence, it is safe to conclude that those who applied this term to Mary regarded her as able to ensure the protective care of God himself. In this belief, the early Christians anticipated the later teaching of the Church, as seen in the following words from the Introduction to Mass 39 of the *Collection of Masses of the Blessed Virgin Mary*:

"The title 'Queen of Mercy' celebrates the kindness, the generosity, the dignity of the Blessed Virgin, who from her place in heaven fulfills the role of Queen Esther (Esther 4:17), 'never ceasing to pray' to her Son for the salvation of her people as they confidently fly to her for refuge in their trials and dangers.

"The Blessed Virgin is thus the 'gracious' and 'compassionate' Queen 'who has herself uniquely known God's loving kindness and stretches out her arms to embrace all who take refuge in her'; hence she is rightly addressed as 'solace of the repentant, hope of the distressed.'

"The title 'Mother of Mercy' ... is a fitting title of our Lady both because she brought forth for us Jesus Christ, the visible manifestation of the mercy of the invisible God, and because she is the Spiritual Mother of the faithful, full of grace and mercy.... From her place in heaven [she] points out the needs of the faithful to her Son, with whom she interceded on earth on behalf of the bridegroom and bride of Cana."

SECOND LINE: DIVINE MOTHERHOOD

The next line (*"O holy Mother of God"*) gives the basic reason for Mary's power and for our recourse to her — she is the Mother of God! She has the ear of God. Who could fear if the Mother of God is behind us!

St. Germanus expands slightly on these words: "O Mary, you possess the authority of a Mother toward God. Therefore, it is impossible for you not to be heard, for God always treats you like his true and immaculate Mother."

St. Louis de Montfort adds a few more details on the subject: "The Son of God,... by making himself entirely subject to Mary as his Mother, gave her a maternal and natural authority over himself which surpasses our understanding. He not only gave her this power while he lived on earth but still gives it now in heaven, because glory does not destroy nature but makes it more perfect....

"As his Mother, Mary has authority over Jesus, who because he wills it, remains in a sense subject to her. This means that Mary, by her powerful prayers and because she is the Mother of God, obtains from Jesus all she wishes. It means that she gives him to whom she decides, and produces him every day in the souls of those he chooses."

As noted above, this phrase is also a precious witness to the use of the term Mother of God by Christians before the fourth century.

In the Preface (P 13) for the Mass of the Commending of the Blessed Virgin in the *Collection of Masses* already mentioned, the Church sets forth the corollary to Mary being "Mother of God" — she is also "Mother of those who believe."

"At the foot of the Cross of Jesus, by his solemn and dying wish, a deep bond of love is fashioned between the Blessed Virgin Mary and his faithful disciples: the Mother of God is entrusted to the disciples as their own Mother, and they receive her as a precious inheritance from their Master.

"She is to be for ever the Mother of those who believe, and they will look to her with great confidence in her unfailing protection. She loves her Son in loving her children, and in heeding what she says they keep the words of their Master."

THIRD LINE: REQUEST FOR HELP IN NEED

Using the third line (*"Despise not our petitions in our necessities"*), the supplicants beg Mary not to despise (that is, set aside) their plea uttered in a time of desperate need. They ask Mary to be a real protector, not like those who claim to protect them in the abstract and then turn aside when the concrete need arises.

For Christians, the most important necessities in life are spiritual ones. This plea takes that fact for granted and could well recall the words of St. Alphonsus Liguori: "The Motherly Heart of Mary has a great desire to give us grace. This desire is even greater than our desire to receive grace!"

The Preface (P 29) of the Mass of the Blessed Virgin, Queen of All Creation in the *Collection of Masses* nicely sums up the teaching that is behind this petition:

"When the Blessed Virgin, your lowly handmaid, endured with patient suffering the shame of her Son's crucifixion, you exalted her above all the choirs of angels to reign with him in glory and *to intercede for all your children, our advocate of grace* and the queen of all creation."

FOURTH LINE: MARY OUR DELIVERER

The fourth line (*"But deliver us always from all dangers"*) takes it for granted that Mary is all powerful and will not refuse to heed our petitions. Hence, it follows that she will be able to save her supplicants in any danger. All she needs to do is will it and ask her Son to help.

This simple but powerful plea is fleshed out by St. Augustine: "Through Mary, the miserable obtain mercy, the graceless find grace, and sinners receive pardon. The weak gain strength, earthlings acquire heavenly things, mortals win life, and pilgrims reach their homeland!"

The Introduction to the Mass of Our Lady of Ransom (No. 43 in the *Collection of Masses*) offers a deeper look at this role of Mary:

"Our Lady is... *a new Judith*: just as the first Judith courageously freed her people from the siege by Holofernes, so Mary in her warfare against the serpent, the ancient enemy, brought blessings on the people of Israel and on the whole Church....

"[She is] *a loving Mother*, given to us by God in his mercy, one who cares unceasingly with a Mother's love for all God's children in their need, *breaking the chains of every form of captivity, that we might enjoy full liberty of body and spirit.*"

FIFTH LINE: MARY'S DESIRE AND POWER TO ACT

The prayer concludes on a note of spiritual understanding and reverence in line five (*"O glorious and blessed Virgin"*). Not only is Mary the Mother of God; she is also "in glory" and a "blessed" Virgin. This further reinforces the petitioners' trust in her *power* to help as well as in her *desire* to do so.

This phrase might well have anticipated the words about Mary in glory uttered by St. Pius X: "Mary sits at the right hand of Jesus like a Queen. She is the most safe refuge and the most fruitful helper of all who are in danger; so there is no reason to fear."

The Second Vatican Council gave a careful explanation of the meaning and force of Mary's mediation from her place in glory:

"The maternal role of Mary in relation to the human family

in no way obscures or lessens the unique mediation of Christ but rather demonstrates its power. Any saving influence of the Blessed Virgin on men and women is due not to any intrinsic necessity but to *God's good pleasure.*

"It flows from the superabundance of Christ's merits, is founded on his mediation, is entirely dependent on it, and from it derives its whole efficacy. It does not in any way impede but rather fosters the immediate union of the faithful with Christ" (*Constitution on the Church*, no. 60).

A Prayer for Our Time

This beautiful and time-tested prayer is still one of the few texts to which the Church specifically attaches indulgences. The *Handbook of Indulgences* assigns a partial indulgence for its recitation.

Indeed, the Second Vatican Council alluded to the *Sub Tuum* in the magnificent chapter on Mary in the *Constitution on the Church* (no. 66): "Clearly from earliest times the Blessed Virgin has been honored under the title of *Mother of God*, and the faithful *have taken refuge under her protection in all their dangers and necessities.*"

A case can also be made for the thought that the *Sub Tuum* fits in quite well with the frenetic pace of modern life and the dangerous times in which we live. By making use of it often in our busy lives, we will be carrying out the explicit desire of the Church:

"Let the entire body of the faithful pour forth persevering prayer to the Mother of God and Mother of humankind. Let them implore that she who aided the beginning of the Church by her prayers may now, exalted as she is in heaven above all the Saints and Angels, intercede with her Son in the fellowship of all the Saints" (*Ibid.*, no. 69).

4

The Akathist Hymn

AN OUTSTANDING LITURGICAL HYMN

*T*he Akathist Hymn is an outstanding liturgical text of the Eastern Church, a lengthy poetic composition masterfully arranged to celebrate the mystery of the Mother of God. In keeping with the nature of Liturgy — which is, among other things, the experience of the sacred and invests the whole person (body and soul, mind and heart) to lead us to superhuman communion with the Divine — this marvelous extract from the Liturgy of Praise is intended to live an ecclesial moment of mystical experience in celebration of Mary.

It is unquestionably one of the most beautiful Marian Hymns of all time, a literary monument of the first rank, and a liturgical masterpiece of ecclesial importance. As such, it is equivalent to a "contemplative" prayer.

This Hymn bears a singular title — stemming from a liturgical rubric transformed into a proper name. In Greek, the term *akathistos* means "not sitting," that is, "standing." Hence, it is a case of a Hymn that contrary to the other liturgical Eastern hymns is to be sung and listened to *on one's feet* like the Gospel — as a sign of external as well as internal reverence for the Incarnation of the Son of God announced by the Angel.

Originally composed for the Annunciation, the Akathist Hymn is sung in its entirety in the Byzantine Office for the Fifth Saturday of Lent, which is known as the "Saturday of the Akathist." It is also celebrated partially on the preceding four Saturdays of Lent.

The most recent studies place the date of composition in the second half of the fifth century or the first half of the sixth. Its author is unknown though it has been attributed to George of Pisidia (d. 630), the Patriarch Sergius (630-638), St. Germanus of Constantinople (d. 733), or most often to St. Romanos the Melodist (d. 556).

However, scholars maintain that neither Romanos nor any other sacred hymnographer reached the heights found in the Akathist Hymn. They assert that the author was a great poet, a master theologian, and a consummate contemplative. Such was his greatness that he was able to express in a praying synthesis the faith that the Church professes; at the same time, such was his humility that he chose to remain anonymous.

The Akathist Hymn is an alphabetic acrostic of 24 stanzas, each of which begins with a letter of the Greek alphabet. The stanzas are divided into two parts of 12 stanzas each. The first 12 are historical; the second 12 are theological. The first 12 stanzas follow the Gospel account from the Annunciation to the meeting with Simeon. The second 12 deal with articles of faith concerning Mary.

The Hymn is further divided into another two groups of 12 — one group of 12 longer stanzas and another of 12 shorter stanzas. The longer (odd-numbered) ones give a historical or thematic introduction and are prolonged by 12 acclamations to the Blessed Virgin concluding with the words "Rejoice, Virgin and Bride." The shorter (even-numbered) stanzas give historical or theological insights about the Incarnation or about Mary's part in it.

OUTLINE OF THE HYMN

The following analysis is based on that of the Italian Mariologist and Patrologist, Fr. Ermanno Toniolo, with some variations.

The first part of the Hymn (stanzas 1-12) follows the Infancy Gospels (Mt 1-2; Lk 1-2) and sets forth and comments on the theophany (the appearance and first historical revelation) of God in human flesh together with the salvific effects stemming from it.

The first six stanzas (1-6) have a Christological character and sing of the descent of the Word and his manifestation to the first witnesses: the Virgin Mother, the Baptist, Elizabeth, and Joseph.

The next six stanzas (7-12) have an ecclesial character and show the epiphany of God in the world that brings light and grace for all. The participants and beneficiaries are the shepherds, the Magi, those redeemed from bondage to idols, that is, the pagan peoples, and the just Simeon, the type of Israel's expectation.

The second part of the Hymn (stanzas 13-24) sets forth the Marian theology of the ancient Church, that is, the profession of the dogmas of faith that concern Mary. The first six stanzas (13-18) contemplate her immersed in the Mystery of Christ. The second six stanzas (19-24) celebrate her presence in the active Mystery of the Church.

For a greater appreciation of this magnificent prayer, the following detailed summary of the contents of each stanza may be helpful.

STANZAS 1-6: DESCENT OF THE WORD

1. God sends his Angel to pronounce the salutation, and the Mystery is completed in Mary. Joy breaks out, the ancient condemnation is overturned, and creation is renewed:

"Rejoice, for through you joy rings out again. Rejoice, for through you sorrow is put to flight. Rejoice, O resurrection of fallen Adam. Rejoice, O redemption of the tears of Eve.... Rejoice, for through you all creation is renewed. Rejoice, for through you the Creator became a Child."

2. Mary registers wonder — the creature is confronted with the mysterious initiatives of God. Mary tells the Angel: "The paradox of your word seems incomprehensible to me."

3. In the face of a hidden Mystery, the question rises spontaneously: "How?" Mary earnestly asks: "Tell me, can my virginal womb ever give birth to a child?" The Angel replies and reveals that she alone is so deeply initiated into the experience of the Divine as to become a guide to human uplifting:

"Rejoice, O guide to the Divine Wisdom. Rejoice, O proof of the hidden Mystery.... Rejoice, O heavenly stairway through whom God came down. Rejoice, O bridge joining earthlings to heaven."

4. The Holy Spirit comes down and overshadows the Virgin, changing her womb into virgin earth fecund with grace: "That womb, made fertile from on high, becomes a fount of salvation for all."

5. Mary goes to visit Elizabeth and upon her salutation the Mystery is revealed to John the Baptist who leaps for joy in Elizabeth's womb. Forgiveness flourishes and mercy is poured forth with Mary as the mediatrix and the altar:

"Rejoice, O table who produce fullness of gifts.... Rejoice, O pleasing incense of prayer. Rejoice, O gracious forgiveness for the whole world. Rejoice, O mercy of God for all peoples. Rejoice, O assurance of human beings before God."

6. The Mystery is revealed to Joseph, the virginal "witness": "Learning that your Motherhood was of the Holy Spirit, he exulted: Alleluia!"

STANZAS 7-12: EPIPHANY OF GOD

7. The shepherds come to adore the newborn Child. They prefigure the Apostles, pastors, and martyrs who throughout the centuries would announce and profess Christ, born of the Virgin, who as she invested the Lord with flesh clothes the faithful with glory:

"Rejoice, for through you heaven exults with earth. Rejoice, for through you the earth sings out with heaven. Rejoice, O tireless voice of the Apostles. Rejoice, O invincible courage of the martyrs.... Rejoice, for through you we are clothed with glory."

8. The Magi arrive. Those who receive the announcement of faith preached by the shepherds start out to seek God. There begins the catechumenal journey that will end in Mary, from whom the Word of the Father became flesh: "They reach the Inaccessible One and, filled with joy, they cry out to him: Alleluia!"

9. The Magi adore the Child. The catechumenal journey of human beings concludes with the renunciation of Satan and vice and the joyous adherence to the only Lord. The architect and star of this journey is the Mother of God:

"Rejoice, for through your splendor you lead us to the triune God.... Rejoice, for you have ransomed us from barbarous superstitions. Rejoice, for you have saved us from the works of darkness. Rejoice, O guide of believers to Wisdom. Rejoice, O joy of all the nations."

10. The Magi return to their own country and become heralds of Christ by their lives: "The Magi become heralds of God along the way of their return. They proclaim you, O Christ, to all!"

11. Christ enters Egypt, as Isaiah (19:1) had foretold, carried by Mary. The idols crumble and in his wake begins the exodus of the new people toward the promised land:

"Rejoice, O sea who engulf the Pharaoh supreme. Rejoice, O rock who pour forth water to quench those thirsty for life. Rejoice,

O pillar of fire who guide in darkness. Rejoice, O cloud of a world larger than the firmament. Rejoice, O giver of the heavenly manna. Rejoice, O minister of the holiest of foods. Rejoice, O mystical promised land. Rejoice, O torrent of milk and honey."

12. The Child Jesus encounters Simeon. Human expectation and wisdom are illumined in Christ: "You were given to him under the aspect of a Child, but in you Simeon discerned the God of perfection."

STANZAS 13-18:
MARY'S POWER IN THE MYSTERY OF CHRIST

13. The virginal conception takes place. With this new prodigy life is reborn. The holiness and virginal obedience of the new Eve are contrasted with the ancient disobedience and cancel it, reconciling the world with God:

"Rejoice, O flower of a life uninterrupted.... Rejoice, for you unveil the life of Angels.... Rejoice, O pacifier of the Just Judge. Rejoice, O pardon for all who are lost. Rejoice, O welcome garment for those deprived of grace. Rejoice, O love who overcome all covetousness."

14. In Christ, human beings return to the origins. In the Incarnate Word, the heavens open to them: "Contemplating the wondrous birth we detach our thoughts from earth and raise them to heaven."

15. The Divine Motherhood is the supreme vertex, throne of God, and the sole path by which pardoned human beings become "Divine":

"Rejoice, O seat of the infinite God.... Rejoice, O throne more holy than the throne of the Cherubim.... Rejoice, for through you the bonds of the fault were loosened. Rejoice, for through you heaven's gates were flung wide.... Rejoice, O hope of eternal things."

16. Even for the Angels, the Mystery of the Word Incarnate constitutes new light for understanding and ecstasy: "For they saw the God who is inaccessible to all made accessible and human."

17. The virginal childbirth is an abyss of Divine Wisdom. The light of human wisdom resides in the faith of the simple, which finds its light in Mary:

"Rejoice, O vessel of the Divine Wisdom.... Rejoice, for you reveal the ignorance of the wise. Rejoice, for through you the most subtle scholars are seen to be fools.... Rejoice, for you protect us against the abyss of ignorance. Rejoice, O beacon of understanding for all."

18. If God had not come down humbly among us to save and draw us sweetly to himself, we could never have approached him: "As God he was our shepherd, but he wished to appear among us as a Lamb: through the human he attracted humans; as God he hears us acclaim him: alleluia!"

STANZAS 19-24:
MARY'S PRESENCE IN THE MYSTERY OF THE CHURCH

19. Mary's perpetual virginity is the beginning of the holy Church and the sublime model for virgins. In her womb Mary espoused God to human beings and now she leads virgins and espouses them to the Word of God:

"Rejoice, O column of holy purity.... Rejoice, O firstfruits of a new spiritual progeny.... Rejoice, for you have given wisdom to those lacking it.... Rejoice, for you give us the Author of chastity. Rejoice, O bosom of the Divine nuptials.... Rejoice, O gentle nurse of virgins. Rejoice, O bringer of souls to the Spouse."

20. The first duty of virgins is the worship of God. Human beings are incapable of worthily celebrating the Divine benefits no matter how long they prolong their praise: "Even if we offered as many hymns as there are grains of sand, O Lord, it would never be enough for the gifts you give us."

21. Mary also has a spiritual motherhood. She is the "Mother of the Church." Just as she has generated the Head according to the flesh so she does not cease to regenerate the members in him by means of the Sacraments that infuse light and life:

"Rejoice, for you are the fount of the sacred Mysteries for us.... Rejoice, for you are the source of many waters.... Rejoice, for you take away the stains of our sins. Rejoice, O fount who cleanse consciences. Rejoice, O cry who spread gladness. Rejoice, O fragrance of the chrism of Christ. Rejoice, O life of the mystical banquet."

22. Our regeneration stems from the Paschal Mystery, which has its roots in the virginal womb. For our salvation, Christ came down from heaven and became incarnate by Mary the Virgin: "Wishing to pardon every ancient debt, the Redeemer came among us and dwelled among us in person."

23. Mary now carries out a function of mediation in heaven. Our Lady is Temple and Ark who accompanies and protects the pilgrim Church in the holy conquest of the heavenly homeland: "Singing a hymn to your giving birth, the universe exalts you as the living Temple, O *Theotokos*":

"Rejoice, O Tabernacle of the Word of God.... Rejoice, O Ark made golden by the Spirit.... Rejoice, O venerable glory of saintly priests. Rejoice, O invincible rampart for the Church.... Rejoice, for through you we raise our standards. Rejoice, for through you our enemies are defeated. Rejoice, O health of my members. Rejoice, O salvation of my soul."

24. Mary is our Advocate. The Mother of God saves us from every danger and from all punishment.

A Hymn To Be Used

It may not be out of place to hope that this contemplative prayer-hymn will be come to be used and appreciated by many of our Western faithful. It constitutes both a wonderful paean of praise to the Mother of God and a treasury of authentic Marian teaching.

The Akathist Hymn accurately portrays Mary as present and operative wherever the Mystery of the Word made flesh is. Wherever the humanity of Christ is fount of life, there is Mary who gave him flesh; there is Mary in her aspect as virgin and in her action as mother.

Mary's virginity was a mission of peace that the Lord accepted in favor of a fallen world and that led him to become one of us. Her Divine fecundity bestowed a Redeemer on the erring, canceled the ancient condemnation, despoiled hell of its prey, flung open the gates of heaven, and united all people in one single praise. As Mary was the heavenly ladder through whom the Lord came down, so she is the bridge bringing all human beings to heaven.

The Hymn shows vividly that, today like yesterday, the Blessed Virgin is an operative presence in the pilgrim Church. She is the sustenance of faith, the word of the Apostles, and the strength of martyrs. For they all announce and bear witness to Christ, whom she gave us. It also stresses that Mary has been present to the Church from the beginning in the Paschal Mystery and is always present along the Church's pilgrimage to the true homeland. She is the column of light illuminating the way, the propitious cloud protecting the way, the surging fountain giving refreshment with the water of life, the table offering the bread from heaven, the earth cultivated by the holy people, and the port where the course of humankind leads.

The Akathist Hymn is worth contemplating over and over for its riches are manifold and not easily assimilated by one reading. The more we make use of it the more we return to it with renewed joy and understanding. And the more we marvel at the theological wisdom, deep faith, and poetic artistry of the author of this greatest of liturgical prayers to our Lady.

5

Final Antiphons of Our Lady

BRIEF HISTORY

*A*s the fifth Great Marian Prayer in this series it is fitting that we make use of a double prayer comprising the first two of the four final antiphons of our Lady recited or sung at the end of Night Prayer in the *Liturgy of the Hours*:

Alma Redemptoris Mater (AHL-mah ray-dem-TAWH-rees MAH-ter) ("Loving Mother of the Redeemer") and *Ave, Regina Caelorum* (AH-vay ray-JEE-nah chay-LAWH-room) ("Hail, Queen of Heaven").

The other two antiphons that made up this select group of Marian antiphons will be treated later in this volume: chapter 6: Hail, Holy Queen (*Salve Regina* — SAHL-vay ray-JEE-nah) and chapter 8: *Regina Caeli* (ray-JEE-nah CHAY-lee) ("Queen of Heaven").

Until the *Liturgy of the Hours* was promulgated, each of these four traditional rhymed prayers or antiphons was specified for a certain liturgical season. The *Alma Redemptoris Mater* was used from Advent to February 2 inclusive; the *Ave Regina Caelorum* from February 2 to Holy Thursday exclusive; the *Regina Caeli* during Easter Time; and the *Salve Regina* from Trinity Sunday to Advent.

The origin of these final antiphons has been traced to Jordan of Saxony, the second Master General of the Dominicans, after the death of St. Dominic in 1221. In order to put an end to troublesome incidents that had arisen in the Convent at Bologna, Jordan ordered that every day after Night Prayer (Compline) the *Hail, Holy Queen* should be sung. This antiphon had been introduced into the Liturgy by Adhemar of Monteil in the eleventh century.

The custom spread to other religious houses, and the other three Marian antiphons were soon added. In 1249, John of Parma mentions that the Franciscan Order chanted one of the four antiphons after Night Prayer according to the liturgical seasons as indicated above. This custom was made part of the *Roman Breviary* when it was issued by Pope Pius V in 1568.

In the revised *Breviary* of Vatican II, known as the *Liturgy of the Hours*, the four antiphons were retained but made optional for any season. Furthermore, in the English edition, only three of the antiphons are kept in both English and Latin; the *Ave Regina Caelorum* has, for some reason, been eliminated.

It is believed that these Marian Antiphons started out as antiphons to be recited or sung around a psalm. Possibly because of their beautiful musical renditions as well as their depth of spiritual thought, they became very popular. In time, they entered the ordinary prayer life of Christians.

In recent years, these antiphons — especially the two being treated today — are not as well known to Catholics as they once were. Yet they have lost none of their spiritual power or beauty.

ALMA REDEMPTORIS MATER

The *Alma Redemptoris Mater* is probably the better known of the two. Anyone who has ever heard its most famous Latin rendition in chant is hardly apt to forget it.

This beloved prayer, whose title comes from the first three words of its original Latin version, is ascribed to Herman the Cripple, a monk of Richenau (1013-1054). As can be expected, there are many English versions of the six hexameters in which it is written. The following is one of them.

> *Mother benign of our redeeming Lord,*
> *Star of the sea and portal of the skies,*
> *Unto your fallen people help afford —*
> *Fallen, but striving still anew to rise.*
>
> *You who did once, while wondering worlds adored,*
> *Bear your Creator. Virgin then as now,*
> *Pity the sinners who before you bow.*

MOTHER OF OUR REDEEMER

The *Alma Redemptoris Mater* is said to utilize expressions taken from St. Fulgentius, St. Epiphanius, St. Irenaeus, and Sedulius. It sings the praises of Mary as the Mother of our Redeemer, who was also the Son of God. It is a reminder that she conceived and brought forth, in his human nature, the One who is God from all eternity.

In ordinary human generation, the terminus of the parents' generative action is the person subsisting in the human nature produced. So in Mary's case her maternal action reaches the Person of the Word. By this very fact, he is truly her Son.

As A. Delesalle has written, "Mary is Mother of the Redeemer in a sense much more profound than when we say of a woman that she is mother of a priest or of the president of a nation. The fact of being a priest or president of a nation does not result from the generative action of the parents but from a call or a consecration or an election, which affects a person already 'humanly' constituted....

"The engendering to which Mary is called, with all the spiritual and physical resources of her being, could not but produce, ontologically and existentially, the Mediator par excellence, whom she for her part is instrumental in constituting as such. This also indicates the depth of the association that exists here between Mary and the Holy Spirit, who alone is capable of realizing in her such a wonder."

At the same time, Mary is not only the ever-Virgin Mother of our Redeemer but our Mother as well. It was from the Cross that Jesus gave Mary to us as our Mother when he said to the Apostle John (who symbolized us): "Behold your Mother" (John 15:26).

Mary is the Mother of all human beings because Christ died for all. As the Second Vatican Council indicated, Mary received the Word of God into her heart and her body at the Angel's announcement and thereby *brought life to the world.*

She conceived in her heart, with her whole being, before she conceived in her womb. First came Mary's faith and then her Motherhood. By her faith she became the perfect example of what the Gospels mean by "spiritual Motherhood."

"Mary conceived, brought forth, and nourished Christ. She presented him to the Father in the Temple and was united with him by compassion as he died on the Cross. In this singular way, she cooperated by her obedience, faith, hope, and burning charity in the work of the Savior in giving back supernatural life to souls. Therefore, she is our Mother in the order of grace" (*Constitution on the Church,* no. 61).

The purpose of Mary's maternal activity is to unite us with Christ so completely that each of us may say: "The life I live is no longer my own; it is Christ living in me" (Galatians 2:20).

Thus, she is our "Star of the sea" pointing out the Divine way to us on our earthly pilgrimage through life as well as the "Portal of the skies" ushering us into heaven at our death. Afflicted with the weakness resulting from original sin, we cry out to our Mother, and from heaven "she... continues to bring us the gifts of eternal salvation by her constant intercession" (*Ibid.,* no. 62).

ASSOCIATE OF THE REDEEMER

This prayer takes for granted the truth that Mary is the *Associate* of the Redeemer. This term is a modern one, used by Pope Pius XII in place of the word Coredemptrix:

Mary is the "noble Associate of the Divine Redeemer" (*Apostolic Constitution on the Assumption*).

Together with Christ (*although in complete subordination to him and by reason of his power*), Mary atoned or satisfied for the sins of the human race, merited every grace for the salvation of all human beings, and united herself with the Redeemer's sacrifice on Calvary to satisfy God's justice.

The Second Vatican Council called Mary the "generous Associate" of the Lord (*Constitution on the Church*, no. 61). In this same text, it set forth three important points about Mary as Associate.

(1) She cooperated *in a special way* in the work of the Redeemer. (2) She was not a mere passive instrument in God's hands but cooperated in the salvation of the world *with free faith and obedience*. (3) She is truly the *Mother of the members of Christ* because she cooperated with Christ in the birth of the faithful in the Church, who are members of her Head. Thus, she is the Virgin Mother of Christ just as the Church is the Virgin Mother of all the faithful.

In short, Mary is actively associated with Christ the Redeemer in the work of the salvation of the world in a *universal, integral, and completely dependent manner*.

This title reminds us that we too can somehow take part in Christ's redemption. With Mary we can be "associates" of Christ every hour of all our days. All we need do is to fill them with prayer, conscientious works, and kindness toward all we encounter as well as to offer up the trials that each day brings.

In this way we will also be doing what St. Paul the Apostle intimated should be done — making our sufferings "fill up" the sufferings of Christ: "I rejoice now in the sufferings I bear for your sake; and I fill up in my flesh what is lacking in the sufferings of Christ for his Body, which is the Church" (Colossians 1:24).

AVE REGINA CAELORUM

The *Ave Regina Caelorum*, whose title comes from the first three Latin words, is composed of eight short verses of iambic metric diameters of eight syllables each. It reproduces some of the finest praises addressed to the "Queen of Heaven" in the old Testament ("A shoot will spring from the root of Jesse" — Isaiah 11:1; "This gate will be closed" — Ezekiel 44:2) and in the Fathers.

Dating from the twelfth century, it has been attributed to St. Bernard, but its author is unknown. The following English translation is one of many.

> *Hail, O queen of Heaven enthroned!*
> *Hail, by angels Mistress owned!*
> *Root of Jesse, Gate of morn,*
> *Whence the world's true Light was born.*
> *Glorious Virgin, joy to you,*
> *Loveliest whom in heaven they view:*
> *Fairest where all are fair,*
> *Plead with Christ our sins to spare.*

QUEEN OF HEAVEN

Mary is hailed as the Queen of Heaven, of Angels and all human beings. She is the "Root of Jesse" and "the Gate of morn," the Mother of the true Light of the world. In our day, the Church has brought forth the *Order of Crowning an Image of the Blessed Virgin Mary*, which has much to tell us about Mary's Queenship.

In the plan of God, Christ's abasement is followed by his exaltation at the Father's right hand. This Paschal Mystery (abasement-exaltation) is prolonged in the members of Christ, especially Mary his Mother and perfect follower.

Mary's Queenship stems from her humility and abasement. When we see Mary crowned, we must also keep in mind the modest character of her life on earth. Therefore, it becomes clear that the God who has exalted Mary — a lowly and poor woman, faithful to his Word — will also exalt those on earth who are persecuted and humiliated because of their fidelity to the Gospel.

Mary's Queenship is one not of pomp and power but of love and service in the same way that Christ's Kingdom is described by the Gospel: "My Kingdom does not belong to this world" (John 18:36); "the Son of Man has come not to be served by others but to serve, to give his own life as a ransom for the many" (Matthew 20:28).

The new rite makes the reasons for Mary's Queenship crystal clear. She deserves to be Queen because she is: (1) the Mother of the Son of God and the Messiah King (cf. Luke 1:30-32); (2) the loving Associate of the Redeemer who made us a Kingdom to our God (cf. Revelation 5:10); (3) the perfect follower (or disciple) of Christ, who was taken up into heavenly glory and exalted by the Lord as Queen of all (*Constitution on the Church*, no. 59); and (4) the most excellent member of the Church, who is rightly invoked as Queen of Angels and of Saints, as our Lady and our Queen.

ADVOCATE OF GRACE

The second part of the *Ave Regina Caelorum* clearly indicates that Mary is our Advocate of Grace. Advocate is a title that was given her from the earliest of times. Already in the early part of the third century, St. Irenaeus described her as the "advocate of Eve."

In his eyes, the term has the same meaning as it has today when applied to a lawyer — "someone who defends." However, Mary's defense of Eve is not to be taken literally as a personal act of intercession on behalf of Eve.

Rather it refers to the action that Mary, adhering with faith and obedience to God's plan, accomplishes in favor of the human race. This action of Mary, which rectifies and annuls the consequences of Eve's unbelief and disobedience, constitutes a true defense of Eve. She can no longer be accused of the ruin that fell upon the human race because that ruin has been dispelled thanks to Mary's obedience.

St. Bernard stated that the Eternal Father, wishing to show all the mercy possible, besides giving us Jesus as our principal Advocate with him, also gave us Mary as our Advocate with Jesus:

"There is no doubt that Jesus is the only Mediator of justice between human beings and God. By virtue of his merits and promises, he can and will obtain for us pardon and Divine favors.

"But because human beings recognize in him the majesty of God, since he *is* God and because they fear his Divine Majesty, it was necessary to assign us another Advocate to whom we can appeal with less fear and more confidence. This Advocate is Mary."

We can always have recourse to her with confidence, for she will defend us! In the words of St. Thomas of Villanova:

"This Great Mother, who is the Mother of your God and Judge, is also the Advocate for the whole human race. Moreover, she is the proper person for this office, because she can do with God whatever she wills.

"She is all-wise, for she understands all the ways to appease him. And her solicitude is really universal, in the sense that she welcomes everybody and refuses to defend no one."

Thus, Mary, besides testifying to our ultimate future with Christ, cooperates to bring it into effect in us. In relation to us who are enmeshed in the weaknesses of the world, she is constituted as an intercessor.

The Second Vatican Council endorsed this view of Mary as Advocate and then cautioned: "This, however, is to be understood in such a way that it neither takes away from nor adds anything to the dignity and efficaciousness of Christ the one Redeemer" (*Constitution on the Church*, no. 62).

In other words, Jesus, who is all-powerful, has also made Mary all-powerful. However, it is always true that Jesus is all-powerful by *nature* while Mary is all-powerful only by *grace*.

6

The Hail, Holy Queen

BRIEF HISTORY OF THE PRAYER

The *Hail, Holy Queen* (in Latin: *Salve Regina*, i.e., SAHL-vay ray-JEE-nah) is one of the most widely used prayers to our Lady, owing to its tender devotional language and the beautiful plainsong setting to which it is sung in Latin. This jewel of praise and supplication was even recited after Mass between 1884 and 1964. And it is said to have been recited by the crew of Christopher Columbus just before he admonished his sailors to look for land the evening before the New World was sighted.

This prayer is still recited (or sung) in the official Prayer of the Church (the *Liturgy of the Hours*), and some people add it to the end of their Rosary.

The author of this beloved prayer, which dates from the eleventh century, is unknown. It may have been Herman the Cripple (1013-1054) or Bishop Adhemar of Le Puy (d. 1098), one of the proponents of the First Crusade.

It was introduced into the liturgical services of the Abbey of Cluny about 1135. Later the Cistercians made use of it and then the Dominicans. Since the thirteenth century it has been the last evening chant of many religious communities.

The fourteenth century saw its inclusion in the *Divine Office* (the forerunner of the *Liturgy of the Hours*).

After greeting our Queen and our Mother, who is full of tender love for us, we cry out our needs. For she is our Advocate. We ask that when our time comes she may show us Jesus, who is born of her!

So popular did this prayer become in the Church that St. Alphonsus Liguori devoted a whole book to explaining it — volume I of his phenomenally popular two-volume *Glories of Mary*. (Many of the points below come from this source.)

As is true of all prayers that originated in another language, there are various English translations of this prayer. Perhaps the most known is the one that appeared in the 1969 edition of the *Enchiridion of Indulgences*:

> *Hail, holy Queen, Mother of Mercy;*
> *hail, our life, our sweetness, and our hope.*
> *To you do we cry, poor banished children of Eve.*
> *To you do we send up our sighs,*
> *mourning and weeping in this valley of tears.*
> *Turn then, most gracious Advocate,*
> *your eyes of mercy toward us.*
> *And after this our exile*
> *show unto us the blessed fruit of your womb, Jesus.*
> *O clement, O loving, O sweet Virgin Mary.*

LINE 1: QUEEN AND MOTHER

"Hail, holy Queen, Mother of Mercy." We should have great confidence in Mary because she is a *Queen*. St. Thomas Aquinas states: "When the Blessed Virgin conceived the eternal Word in her womb and gave him birth, she obtained half the Kingdom of God. She became Queen of Mercy, and he became King of Justice."

Mary thus opens the abyss of God's mercies to anyone she pleases, when she pleases, and as she pleases. No sinners will be lost when this most holy Lady intercedes for them.

Our Lady is said to have told St. Bridget in a private revelation: "I am the Queen of Heaven and the Mother of Mercy. I am the joy of the just and the door through which sinners come to God. There are no sinners on earth so unfortunate as to be beyond my mercy."

We should have even greater confidence because Mary is our *Mother*. In the words of St. Anselm: "O happy confidence! O perfect refuge! The Mother of God is my Mother. What firm trust we should have, then, since our salvation depends on the judgment of a good Brother and a loving Mother!"

LINE 2: OUR LIFE, SWEETNESS, AND HOPE

"Hail, our life, our sweetness, and our hope." Mary is our *life*: she obtains pardon for our sins and ensures perseverance for us. Just as the soul gives life to the body, so grace imparts life to the soul. Since Mary obtains grace for sinners through her intercession, she restores life to their souls. We can apply the words of Scripture to her: "They who find me find life and win favor from the Lord" (Proverbs 8:35).

Mary is our *sweetness*: she renders death sweet. On that day when Mary had the sad privilege of witnessing the death of her Son Jesus, who was the Head of the elect, she was granted the further privilege of assisting at the death of all the elect themselves.

Hence, our Lady comes and assists us at death and comforts us with her presence, provided only that we serve her with love during our time on earth.

Mary is our *hope*: we trust that through her intercession we will obtain the graces we would not obtain through our unaided prayers. "Hail then, O hope of my soul!" exclaims St. Ephrem of Edessa. "Hail, O sure salvation of Christians; hail, helper of sinners; hail, fortress of the faithful and salvation of the world!"

God has given our Lady to us to be our exemplar, to teach us how to lead good lives, and to be our refuge in all trials and afflictions. Thus, in the words of St. Bernard, "Let those who have no hope hope in Mary!"

LINES 3-5: MARY OUR REFUGE

"To you do we cry. . . . To you do we send up our sighs, mourning and weeping in this valley of tears. Mary comes to the aid of all who invoke her. Indeed, this good Mother's compassion is so great and her love is so urgent that she does not wait for our prayers — she anticipates them. We can apply to her the words of Scripture: "She hastens to make herself known in anticipation of people's desire" (Wisdom 7:13). Her power is great, especially in time of temptation.

Jesus is the only Mediator; by his Death and Resurrection, he has achieved humankind's reconciliation with God. But Jesus is pleased to grant graces at the intercession of Mary his Mother, whom he desires to see loved and honored by all. Hence, Mary is the Mediatrix of our salvation; not a Mediatrix of justice but a Mediatrix of grace and intercession!

In her approved prayers, the Church is always teaching us to have recourse to the Mother of God and to invoke her as Health of the Sick, Refuge of Sinners, Help of Christians, and Our Life and Our Hope.

Our Lady herself wants us to seek her always and invoke her aid. She desires these marks of veneration so that our confidence and devotion may be increased by them and move her to answer us with greater help and comfort.

LINE 6: OUR GRACIOUS ADVOCATE

"Turn, then, most gracious Advocate." Mary is an Advocate with power to save all. The prayers of our Lady are the prayers of a Mother and have in them something of a command; it is impossible for her not to be heard. This leads to the famous saying: "What God can do by commanding, you can do by praying, O Blessed Virgin."

Mary is a compassionate Advocate for even the most wretched of persons. Our Blessed Mother is far more powerful than all the Saints. And to that same degree she is more tender and solicitous for our happiness.

Our Lady is the singular Refuge of the abandoned, the Hope of the miserable, and the Advocate of every sinner who turns to her.

Mary is the peacemaker between sinners and God. In his eagerness to show us mercy God has given us his Son as our Advocate. And then to make our confidence even stronger, he has made available to us another Advocate, who obtains through her prayer whatever she asks.

LINE 7: MARY'S COMPASSION

"Your eyes of mercy toward us." Mary is all eyes to protect and save us. In the Scriptures it says: "The Lord has eyes for the just" (Psalm 34:16). But our Lady has eyes for sinners as well as the just.

St. Bonaventure says: "If Mary's compassion for the miserable was great when she was on earth, it is even greater now. By the countless graces she obtains for us, she proves how much more merciful she has become, being now better acquainted with our miseries."

Our Lady's eyes are a Mother's eyes, and a Mother not only watches her children to keep them from falling but also helps them up if they fall. Mary is the Mother beyond compare, and she constantly watches over us.

LINES 8-9: MARY LEADS US TO JESUS

"And after this our exile show unto us the blessed fruit of your womb, Jesus."
Mary saves her clients from eternal death. Those clients of our Lady who sincerely resolve to do better and are faithful in honoring her and recommending themselves to her can never be lost. Mary has the power and the will to save us, for she is our Mother and desires our salvation more than we can desire it.

St. Anselm says: "It is impossible for persons who recommend themselves to Mary, and are therefore watched over by her, to be lost."

Mary also helps her clients in purgatory. She consoles them and espouses their cause. We should implore our Lady's assistance for them in all our prayers, especially by saying the Rosary for them.

Mary leads her clients to heaven. The Church calls her the Gate of Heaven and the Star of the Sea. Just as sailors are guided to port by a star, so Christians are guided to heaven by Mary.

The Mother of God has already secured heaven for us through her assistance and her prayers. All we need do is put no obstacle in the way. Therefore, those who serve her and enjoy her intercession may be, so to speak, as sure of heaven as if they were already there.

LINE 10: THE WONDERFUL NAME OF MARY

"*O clement, O loving, O sweet Virgin Mary.*" Mary sees and knows our needs far better than we do ourselves. She is more eager to grant her graces than we are to receive them! No wonder when we go to her we find her hands filled with generous mercies. After the Name of Jesus, the Name of Mary is so rich in blessings that there is no other in heaven or earth that brings such peace and hope and sweetness to the devout.

St. Anthony of Padua says: "The name of Mary is joy in the heart, honey in the mouth, and melody in the ears."

We should often make use of this wonderful Marian prayer known as the *Hail, Holy Queen*. Then with St. Bernard we will be able to say:

> O Mary,
> you are clement to those who need you,
> compassionate to those who beseech you,
> and sweet to those who love you!
> You are clement to the penitent,
> compassionate to the virtuous,
> and sweet to the perfect!
> You are clement in working for us,
> compassionate in giving grace,
> and sweet in giving yourself!

7

The Angelus

THREEFOLD DAILY RECITATION

Sunday after Sunday, Pope John Paul II appears at the window of the Apostolic Palace and continues a practice followed by his venerable predecessors. He recites the beautiful Marian prayer known as the *Angelus* (AN-juh-luhs) and a prayer for the faithful departed.

The Pope's *Angelus* is preceded by a short meditation and a remembrance of the events that should be especially recommended to God and is concluded by a blessing. In carrying out this practice the Pope is also reminding us of a long-standing custom that was so dear to clients of our Lady.

Time was when the threefold daily recitation (morning, noon, and evening) of this Marian prayer constituted a way of life for most Catholics. This fact was beautifully captured by J.F. Millet (1814-1875) in his celebrated painting entitled "The Angelus," which is spellbinding in its simplicity and depth of understanding.

The farmer and his wife interrupt their work at the first tolling of the *Angelus* bell. They pause to gain relief from their labor and to recall the one thing necessary, thus putting that labor in perspective.

Today the hurly burly of life has for the most part stilled the tolling of church bells and all but relegated the *Angelus* to oblivion for city Catholics. Yet there is really no need of bells to recite the *Angelus*. And fidelity to its recitation three times a day will immediately result in giving us a deeper understanding of the greatest event in world history and the Christian view of time.

This prayer consists of four verses (each made up of a versicle and a response) plus a concluding prayer. Each of the first three verses is followed by a Hail Mary, and the fourth serves as an introduction to the closing prayer. Its name comes from the first word of the opening versicle in Latin: *Angelus* — "The Angel."

BRIEF HISTORY

From the very beginning of Christianity, the people had a tendency to recite the Angel's Salutation (Hail Mary) to Mary in a cultic context. About the sixth century this Salutation was introduced into the Latin Liturgy at the Offertory Antiphon for the Fourth Sunday of Advent: "Hail, Mary, full of grace, the Lord is with you. Blessed are you among women and blessed is the fruit of your womb."

This paved the way for the *Angelus*, which goes back almost a thousand years and whose development into its present form took place over a series of centuries. Originally, this marvelous prayer was recited only in the morning.

Around the eleventh century, the custom of reciting the Angel's Salutation spread to local churches. In 1197, Bishop Odo of Soliac decreed that his priests should exhort the people "to say the Lord's Prayer, the Creed, and the Salutation of the Blessed Virgin Mary."

In 1263 and 1269, the Franciscan Chapters of Pisa and Assisi instructed the Brothers to have the faithful greet our Lady after the Hour of Compline (Night Prayer) with a Hail Mary and recall the Mystery of the Incarnation at the ringing of the bells. More or less at the same time, Brother Bonvesin of Riva (1260-1315) introduced the ringing of the "Hail Mary bell" in the evening at Milan.

This practice went on to become widespread in Catholic countries. On October 13, 1318, Pope John XXII gave his approval to the custom of reciting the Hail Mary at the hour of curfew. On May 7, 1327, he wrote his Vicar General to have the evening bell of the three Hail Marys rung even in the Eternal City.

Ringing the bell and reciting the Hail Marys also in the evening became established during the fifteenth century. It was especially related to Mary's Sorrows.

The last to be established was the ringing of the bell at midday. King Louis IX of France (d. 1270), who took part in the Seventh and Eighth Crusades, had the "Angelus of Peace" rung at midday. At the toll of the bell, he dismounted from his horse and knelt to pray. In 1456, Pope Callistus III prescribed the daily ringing of the bells at midday with the recitation of three Hail Marys for the success of his Crusade against the Turks.

During the sixteenth century, the various devotions of the *Angelus* were melded into its present form. In 1724, Pope Benedict XII granted a plenary indulgence to all who at the ringing of the bells recited the *Angelus* on their knees.

Eighteen years later, Pope Benedict XIV gave final approval to the devotion and prescribed that during Easter Time the *Angelus* be replaced by another great Marian prayer, the *Regina Caeli* (see chapter 8). Just as the *Angelus* concentrates on the Mystery of the Incarnation, the *Regina Caeli* concentrates on the Mystery of the Resurrection of Christ and his victory over evil, sin, and death.

In 1974, Pope Paul VI added an alternative concluding prayer to the *Angelus*, taken from the Opening Prayer for the Feast of the Annunciation. The usual prayer comes from the Fourth Sunday of Advent.

TEXT OF THE PRAYER

There are actually many English versions of this prayer. Perhaps the most known is the one that appeared in the 1969 edition of the *Enchiridion of Indulgences*:

V. The Angel of the Lord declared unto Mary,
R. And she conceived of the Holy Spirit.
Hail Mary...

V. Behold the handmaid of the Lord.
R. Be it done unto me according to your word.
Hail Mary...

V. And the Word was made flesh,
R. And dwelt among us.
Hail Mary...

V. Pray for us, O holy Mother of God.
R. That we may be made worthy of the promises of Christ.

Let us pray. Pour forth, we beseech you, O Lord,
your grace into our hearts:
that we, to whom the Incarnation of Christ your Son
was made known by the message of the Angel
may by his Passion and Cross
be brought to the glory of his Resurrection
Through the same Christ our Lord.

(Alternative concluding prayer)
O God,
you willed that your Son should truly become Man
in the womb of the Virgin Mary.
We confess that our Redeemer is both God and Man.

Grant that we may deserve to be made like him
in his Divine Nature.

MAJOR THEMES OF THE PRAYER

(1) *Daughter of Zion and Gift of the Spirit.* The first verse refers to Luke 1:26-35. The Angel Gabriel announces the coming of the Savior — the Son of the Most High and the Desired of the Nations — to the "Daughter of Zion," the Woman who incorporates within herself all the expectation of the people of Israel.

The Angel reveals to Mary that she will conceive by the power of the Holy Spirit (cf. Luke 1:35). The Spirit who was at work in the creation of the world and in the rebirth of the ancient People of God now creates in Mary's womb the Humanity of Jesus, the Divine Messiah. And Jesus will accomplish the new creation, which consists in the renewal of the new People of God, whose King and Lord he is — a renewal that will be completed only at his Second Coming.

(2) *The Incarnation of the Word.* The second verse faithfully expresses what is found in Luke 1:38 — Mary's consent to be the Mother of God. It is her positive response to God's invitation that changed the course of the world. This personal decision resulted in Mary becoming the Mother of God and deserving the honor that goes with it.

The third verse comes from the Prologue of John's Gospel (1:14): "And the Word became flesh and dwelt among us," which signals God's intervention in the world. It recalls the fullness of time, when "God sent his Son, born of a woman, born under the law, to ransom those under the law, so that we might receive adoption" (Galatians 4:4-5).

(3) *The intercession of Mary.* The fourth verse is our petition to Mary to pray for us so that we may become worthy to receive the promises of Christ. So great is the power of our spiritual Mother that she can enable us to become fit for adoption by God as brothers and sisters of her Son and heirs of heaven with him.

(4) *The Paschal Mystery.* The two concluding prayers make specific what has been alluded to in the verses. The Incarnation of

the Word opens out to the Paschal Reality — Christ's Passion, Death, and Resurrection. The event of the Incarnation initiated the communion of heaven with earth. The event of the Death and Resurrection reconciles us with God. And just as God requested Mary's collaboration in the first event, in his plan of love he decrees that her collaboration should continue even for the second event — with Mary at the foot of the Cross offering her Son for all humankind (cf. John 19:25-27).

Mary is thus revealed as the "Woman" mentioned in the Book of Genesis (3:15) who would help conquer Satan, the new Jerusalem, the Mother of all believers in Christ — believers who are present in the beloved disciple John standing beneath the Cross of Christ.

RELEVANCE OF THE *ANGELUS*

The *Angelus* is a time-tested and very relevant prayer in our day. Pope Paul VI stated that despite the passing of centuries it "retains an unaltered value and an intact freshness." Indeed, it has no need to be revised since its essential elements are always valid. These are:

(1) *Simple structure*: it includes the announcement of the Angel; the response of Mary; the Incarnation of the Word.

(2) *Biblical character*: it is composed almost wholly out of verses taken from the Gospel.

(3) *Historical origin*: it is linked with the prayer for peace and safety.

(4) *Quasi-liturgical rhythm*: it allows us to sanctify different moments during the day.

(5) *Remembrance of the Paschal Mystery*: it recalls the Incarnation of the Son of God for us and enables us to pray that we may be led through his Passion and Cross to the glory of his Resurrection.

It should be obvious, then, that the *Angelus* is a prayer that we can make good use of during the years of our life on earth. Faithful recitation of it will enable us to honor Mary and at the same time insert us into the Mystery of Jesus. It will lead us *to Jesus through Mary*.

8

The Regina Caeli

A COUNTERPART OF THE ANGELUS

The *Regina Caeli* (ray-JEE-nah CHAY-lee: Latin for "Queen of Heaven") is the counterpart of the *Angelus* during the Easter Season. It is also prescribed in the *Liturgy of the Hours*, especially after Night Prayer from Holy Saturday to the Saturday after Pentecost.

This beloved prayer is an antiphon in honor of the Blessed Virgin Mary written by an unknown author in the twelfth century and imbued with the joy of the Easter Season. It can teach us much about Mary's role in the Paschal Mystery and her role in the life of Catholics.

The structure is quite simple. The corpus is made up of four single lines followed by a versicle and response plus a concluding prayer taken from the Opening Prayer of the Mass for the Common of the Blessed Virgin Mary during the Easter Season.

There are a good many English translations of this prayer both for recited and for sung versions. Perhaps the best known is the one that appeared in the 1969 edition of the *Enchiridion of Indulgences*:

> *Queen of Heaven, rejoice, alleluia:*
> *For he whom you merited to bear, alleluia,*

Has risen, as he said, alleluia.
Pray for us to God, alleluia.

V. *Rejoice and be glad, O Virgin Mary, alleluia.*
R. *Because the Lord is truly risen, alleluia.*

Let us pray.
O God,
who by the Resurrection of your Son,
our Lord Jesus Christ,
granted joy to the whole world:
grant, we beseech you,
that through the intercession of the Virgin Mary, his Mother,
we may lay hold of the joys of eternal life.
Through the same Christ our Lord.

CELEBRATION OF THE PASCHAL MYSTERY

The *Regina Caeli* celebrates Christ's Resurrection as well as Mary's part in it. On three separate occasions Jesus had indicated his Resurrection from the dead (cf. Matthew 16:21-27; 17:22-23; 20:17-19). On Easter morn, he rose as he said he would.

The Resurrection thus leads to the joy of every Christian. In this respect, the prayer conforms with the Entrance Antiphon for Easter Sunday: "I have risen: I am with you once more; you placed your hand on me to keep me safe. How great is the depth of your wisdom, alleluia" (Psalm 139:18, 5-6).

This Easter event leads believers to a union of love with the Risen Lord and an unconquerable joy expressed by the word alleluia. In turn, these give rise to attitudes such as concord, peace, unity, sharing others' joys as well as sufferings, authentic optimism, and zeal to strengthen the spiritual life.

The Easter Season is a manifestation of the ongoing feast of

Easter that must pervade the lives of Christians. We are called to live progressively in time the unique grace of the unique Event, celebrated on the unique Day, and prolonged to the day of the Pentecostal fullness. We can thus see that the Easter Season is the culmination of the entire Liturgical Year.

This reality is beautifully expressed by a passage from the Sermon of St. Augustine commenting on verse 24 of Psalm 117 (118), which is Paschal beyond compare:

"Concerning the words we have just sung to the glory of the Lord: 'This is the day the Lord has made,' we say what he himself wants us to say. The prophetic Scripture indicates that it is not an ordinary day visible to the eyes of the flesh, a day that is born and dies, but a day that has indeed begun but will not end.... This is precisely the day the Lord has made!

"It is a whole day that incorporates both Head and Body: Christ the Head and his Body the Church. This is the day the Lord has made.... Of this day the Apostle says: 'Once you were darkness; but now you are light in the Lord' (Ephesians 5:8). Does he say: 'You were darkness in the Lord'? 'Darkness' in yourselves, indeed, but light in the Lord.

"God 'called the day light' (Genesis 1:2-4): because it is a work of his grace. Human beings of themselves would only be darkness; they were incapable of being light except by work of the Lord. For 'this is the day the Lord has made': the day has not made itself, but God has made it!"

EXPRESSION OF MARY'S QUEENSHIP

Jesus promised to associate his disciples with his own royalty. This applied even more to his Mother and in a special way.

"You who have followed me, in the new creation when the Son of Man is seated on the throne of his glory will also be seated on twelve thrones to judge the twelve tribes of Israel" (Matthew 19:28).

"You are those who have persevered with me in my trials. And I will prepare a Kingdom for you, as the Father has done for me, so that you will eat and drink at my banquet in my Kingdom and be seated on thrones to judge the twelve tribes of Israel" (Luke 22:28-30).

"Behold, I stand at the door and knock. If any hear my voice and open the door, I will come in and dine with them and they with me. I will enable those who overcome to sit beside me on my throne as I have overcome and have sat beside my Father on his throne" (Revelation 3:20-21).

These Scripture texts indicate that only those will receive thrones who follow Christ, heed his voice, and persevere in trials, even to death in order to attain victory.

Mary fulfills these conditions to the fullest degree and so deserves to sit beside Christ as Queen.

From the Annunciation to Pentecost, she espoused the Divine Plan in her own life, listened wholeheartedly to the word of the Son, and carried it out in all kinds of trials even to the supreme hours of desolation on Calvary. Now in union with the whole Church she attains the reward of such fidelity.

Christ lets his Mother sit beside him on his throne (cf. Revelation 3:21). He enables her to share the Divine power he possesses of subjugating all things to himself (cf. Philippians 3:21).

However, in the Divine plan *to reign* means *to serve* (cf. Luke 22:27). Mary becomes Mother of the Messianic King insofar as she declares herself to be the "handmaid of the Lord" (Luke 1:38). And just as the Risen Christ is exalted for having abased himself as the Suffering Servant of the Father, so Mary is given a part in her Son's royal victory for having generously served him in the work of salvation.

Although she is a Queen in heavenly glory, the Mother of Jesus does not cease serving her Son in his followers. She continues to exhort all her children to "do whatever [Jesus] tells you" (John 2:5). By obeying this advice, we can sit at the banquet of the Kingdom wearing nuptial garments (cf. Matthew 22:2, 11-12), with splendid linen robes symbolic of the works of the Saints (cf. Revelation 19:8).

The Second Vatican Council emphasized this serving aspect of Mary's Queenship: "Assumed into heaven, Mary has not set aside this salvific role but with her manifold intercession continues to obtain for us the grace of eternal salvation. With her motherly love she cares for these brothers and sisters of her Son who are still on their earthly pilgrimage until they are led to the heavenly homeland" (*Constitution on the Church*, no. 62).

INSISTENCE ON MARY'S INTERCESSION

The *Regina Caeli* insists on Mary's intercession for us: "Pray for us to God, alleluia." Knowing the suppliant power of the Mother of God to whom her Son wishes to refuse nothing, her children come to her as mendicants.

Pope Pius IX declared in his Bull defining the Immaculate Conception: "Mary intercedes with her Son, in all the power of her Maternal prayer." And Paul VI recalled the "prayerful presence of Mary in the early Church and in the Church throughout all ages; for, having been assumed into heaven, she has not abandoned her mission of intercession and salvation" (*Apostolic Exhortation on Devotion to Mary*, no. 18).

The *Regina Caeli* inspires us to have confidence in Mary's intercession. The reason for this is, of course, that she was and remains totally united with Christ. Devotion to her is a tribute to the power of a Mother over the heart of her Son, but even more it is a recognition of the Blessed Virgin's union with Jesus for the salvation of the world.

There is a twofold basis for the power of Mary's intercession, namely, (1) her union with the work of the Redemption, and (2) the Maternal task entrusted to her, without limits or restrictions. Hence, every new prayer qualifies for presentation by Mary to Jesus. And through Mary's act of uniting it with her Maternal worship, every sincere prayer can be offered in expectation of its being heard.

MARY'S EXAMPLE OF PASCHAL SPIRITUALITY

The *Regina Caeli* also indicates how Mary is our exemplar by her spirituality, which is Paschal: "Rejoice and be glad, O Virgin Mary, alleluia. Because the Lord is truly risen, alleluia."

Christ has saved the world by the Paschal Mystery, and we are to be saved through a spirituality that is Paschal (as the concluding prayer indicates). Our Lady can teach us what such a spirituality means.

Mary lived her participation in the Paschal Mystery in various ways. The Gospel recalls one aspect of Mary's personal experience: in her Motherhood. She experienced the progressive distancing of Jesus from her life as a progressive dying according to the flesh so as to be born according to the spirit.

This separation began with the very birth of Jesus (cf. Luke 2:7). It was accentuated when Jesus as a child demonstrated the independence natural to his youth, but only to carry out tasks assigned him by his heavenly Father (cf. Luke 2:41ff).

It was made final with the baptism at the hand of John the Baptist when Jesus began his public life and had to leave the family home (cf. Luke 3:21ff). At length, this separation was consummated with the Death of Jesus on the Cross, from which he entrusted his Mother to his beloved disciple (cf. John 19:26f).

Mary, for her part, strove to remain united with the Risen Jesus and to conform herself to him. And it was Jesus himself who explicitly invited his Mother to attain this salvific-Paschal Mother-hood. When people told him that his Mother and his brothers and sisters were calling for him (cf. Mark 3:31-32), he said, "My Mother... is the one who does the will of God" (Mark 3:35).

Then dying on the Cross, he indicated that with her partici-pation in his Paschal Mystery Mary had acquired an ecclesial Moth-erhood (cf. John 19:26-27). On entrusting her to John, he made her Mother of the whole Church.

Inasmuch as Mary's spirituality is reached in a singular way through her participation in the Paschal Mystery, she is "evidently the teacher of the spiritual life for individual Christians" (Paul VI: Apostolic Exhortation *Marialis Cultus* on Devotion to Mary, no. 21).

The spiritual life signifies to be open to the Paschal Mystery present to us so as to be "spiritualized" — just as Mary was en-tirely possessed by the Spirit in her essence.

Perhaps St. Louis de Montfort put it best: "I have said that the spirit of Mary is the Spirit of God. In fact, she never let herself be led by her own spirit but always by the Spirit of God, who be-came so much her master as to become the very spirit of Mary" (*Treatise on True Devotion to Mary*, no. 258).

Thus, Mary can teach us how to adhere to God in Christ, so as to become a single spirit with the Lord. She was directed by the Spirit, because already on earth she let herself be animated by the Lord's Paschal Mystery.

By reciting the *Regina Caeli* regularly, we can make this Paschal spirituality a genuine part of our daily life. We can become Spirit-led and ultimately go *to Jesus through Mary.*

9

The Stabat Mater

BOTH SEQUENCE AND HYMN

*T*he *Stabat Mater* (STAH-baht MAH-tuhr) — literally, "The Mother Was Standing" — is the *Sequence* for the Mass of Our Lady of Sorrows (September 15) and a Hymn used in the Office of Readings, Morning Prayer, and Evening Prayer in the *Liturgy of the Hours* for that Memorial. Today it has become one of the greatest prayers to our Lady, especially because of its use in the popular devotion of the Stations of the Cross.

We might define *Sequence* as a syllabic chant in the form of a liturgical poem that originated as a hymn of joy to follow the final note of the Alleluia of the Liturgy of the Word in the Mass. It was originally used to introduce the Gospel for certain important feasts.

Later, Sequences proliferated to such an extent that there are said to have been more than 5,000 during the Middle Ages. The *Roman Missal of Pius V* (carrying out the reforms of the Council of Trent) abolished all but four. The *Roman Missal of Paul VI* retained three of the four (deleting only the *Dies Irae* [DEE-ehs EER-ay] — "Day of Wrath" — used in Masses for the Dead) plus the Sequence

71

for the Mass of the Seven Sorrows of the Blessed Virgin Mary, which had been introduced into the Missal in 1727.

The *Victimae Paschali Laudes* (VIK-tee-may pah-SKAH-lee LOW-des) ("Praise the Paschal Victim") and the *Veni, Sancte Spiritus* (VAY-nee SAHNK-tay SPI-ree-tuhs) ("Come, Holy Spirit") are obligatory in the Masses of Easter and Pentecost respectively; the *Lauda Sion* (LOW-dah SEE-ohn) ("Praise, O Zion") and the *Stabat Mater* ("The Mother Was Standing") are optional in the Masses of the Body and Blood of Christ and Our Lady of Sorrows respectively.

Scholars assert that the Sequence allowed the Middle Ages to inject its own liturgical language and its own liturgical customs into the structure of the Mass. The Sequence along with the Alleluia became, in the words of Joseph Jungmann, "the first crown and climax in the Mass. Here it was that polyphony found its first outlet. At the Sequence the organ seems to have been used as an accompaniment from the start. Later we hear of a solemn pealing of bells to accompany the sequence." With the reform of Pius V, all of this pageantry came to an end.

TEXT OF THE PRAYER

So popular is the *Stabat Mater* that there are some sixty English translations of it. The following is the one found in the Liturgy and the one that is normally used at the Stations of the Cross. Its rhyme scheme is AABCCB for each couplet.

1

At the Cross her station keeping,
Stood the mournful Mother weeping,
   Close to Jesus to the last.
Through her heart, his sorrow sharing,
All his bitter anguish bearing,
   Lo, the piercing sword has passed!

2

O, how sad and sore distressed
Was that Mother highly blessed
Of the sole-begotten One.
Christ above in torment hangs.
She beneath beholds the pangs
Of her dying glorious Son

3

Is there one who would not weep
'Whelmed in miseries so deep
Christ's dear Mother to behold?
Can the human heart refrain
From partaking in the pain
In that Mother's pain untold?

4

Bruised, derided, cursed, defiled,
She beheld her tender Child,
All with bloody scourges rent.
For the sins of his own nation
Saw him hang in desolation
Till his Spirit forth he sent.

5

O sweet Mother! fount of love,
Touch my spirit from above
Make my heart with yours accord.
Make me feel as you have felt.
Make my soul to glow and melt
With the love of Christ, my Lord.

6

Holy Mother, pierce me through.
In my heart each wound renew
  Of my Savior crucified.
Let me share with you his pain,
Who for all our sins was slain,
  Who for me in torments died.

7

Let me mingle tears with [thee],
Mourning him who mourned for me,
  All the days that I may live.
By the Cross with you to stay,
There with you to weep and pray,
  Is all I ask of you to give.

8

Virgin of all virgins blest!
Listen to my fond request:
  Let me share your grief Divine.
Let me to my latest breath,
In my body bear the death
  Of your dying Son Divine.

9

Wounded with his every wound,
Steep my soul till it has swooned
  In his very blood away.
Be to me, O Virgin, nigh,
Lest in flames I burn and die,
  In his awe-full judgment day.

10

Christ, when you shall call me hence,
Be your Mother my defense,
Be your Cross my victory.
While my body here decays,
May my soul your goodness praise,
Safe in heaven eternally.
Amen. Alleluia!

AUTHOR OF THE PRAYER

The *Stabat Mater* has been attributed to Pope Innocent III (d. 1216), or St. Bonaventure (d. 1274), or most often the Franciscan friar Jacopone da Todi (1228-1306). Jacopone was in the line of Franciscans who stressed Mary's compassion and he was filled with love for Christ — indeed, he has been called a fool for Christ. Although he is the object of a popular cultus, he has not been officially beatified.

The tone of the *Stabat Mater* is not very different from the tone of the most beautiful chants of Jacopone — for example, the *Plaint of the Madonna*, which is unquestionably authentic. Here are two verses that, although cursorily translated from the original early Italian, give an idea of the subject matter of the latter poem (which is also known as *Donna del Paradiso* — "Woman of Paradise"):

> *Christ:*
> Mother, why are you crying?
> I want you here remaining,
> and my companions serving —
> those whom on earth I acquired.

Blessed Virgin:
My Son, your word makes me sigh,
For I yearn with you to die
And desire to stay nearby
Till my last breath has expired.

The subject of the *Plaint* like that of the *Stabat Mater* is the compassion of Mary at the Cross. In this sense it follows the Franciscan teaching that was best articulated by St. Bonaventure who preceded Jacopone in the Order by some forty years:

"We must not doubt that the Blessed Mother and Virgin Mary, with a strong heart and unwavering determination, wished to hand over her Son for the salvation of the human race, in such a way that the Mother was completely in conformity with the Father. And what we must greatly praise and admire in her is that she consented that her only Son should be sacrificed for the salvation of the human race.

"Furthermore, she was so united with him in his suffering that if it were possible she would have taken unto herself all the torments that her Son was undergoing. She was therefore at the same time truly strong and tender, sweet and rigorous, parsimonious toward herself but prodigal toward us!

"Hence, it is she who deserves to be loved and venerated above everything after the supreme Trinity and her most holy Son our Lord Jesus Christ, whose Divine Mystery no tongue can succeed in expressing...."

MARY AT THE CROSS (1-2)

The first two couplets give the Scriptural bases for the hymn, especially John 19:25 and Luke 2:34-35. The Church has told us — especially in the Liturgy, including the new *Collection of Masses of the Blessed Virgin Mary* — that our Lady, Queen of heaven and earth, stood by the Cross of her Son in his agony, mournful yet full of courage and faith.

In relation to her Son, she stands there as the Handmaid of the Redeemer, the Mother sharing his sufferings, united with the sacrifice of her Son, the high priest.

She stands there as the new Eve, fulfilling the prophecy of the saving role of the Woman (cf. Genesis 3:15; John 19:26; Revelation 12:1): as the first woman shared in bringing death, so the second woman shares in restoring life.

She also stands there as the Mother of Zion, acclaimed by all peoples as they say: "All find their home in you" (Psalm 87:7), for she welcomes with a Mother's love all who have been scattered but are now gathered into unity by the death of Christ.

Finally, she stands there as the image of the Church, who as she looks upon Mary draws inspiration from her courage and keeps constant faith with her Bridegroom.

HUMAN REACTION TO THE CROSS (3-4)

The third and fourth couplets stress that when we look at Mary standing by the Cross, we cannot but unite with her in her pain. She sees her son "bruised, derided, cursed, defiled,... all with bloody scourges rent" (as depicted in the Passion Accounts).

But once again the Church comes to our aid to help us put this scene in perspective. She tells us that when Mary became the Mother of Christ by the power of the Spirit, she became by a further gift of Divine love a *partner in his Passion*, a Mother suffering with him.

Thus, we rightly celebrate her co-suffering in the drama of salvation because she stood by the Cross firm in faith, strong in hope, and ardent in love. She endured the greatest of pains in bringing forth to new and Divine life the family of the Church, though she had brought forth her Son without pains of childbirth.

Hence, the faithful glorify her as they say: "How blessed was the Virgin Mary in her sufferings: she gained the palm of living martyrdom at the foot of the Cross of her Son" (Communion Antiphon, Mass of the Blessed Virgin Mary at the Foot of the Cross II).

REQUEST TO SHARE MARY'S SUFFERING (5-6)

In the fifth and sixth couplets, the poet has us ask to share Mary's suffering. In doing so he is saying on a natural level what the Church will request from us on a supernatural one. His words are tantamount to asking, on our behalf, to fulfill the sufferings of Christ in keeping with the celebrated passage of Paul: "I fill up in my flesh what is lacking in the sufferings of Christ for his Body, which is the Church" (Colossians 1:24).

The Church tells us that Christ's Passion is mysteriously filled out through the present sufferings of his members as they face the many trials of life. As we share in those sufferings we are to rejoice so that we may be filled with joy when he comes in glory (cf. I Peter 4:13).

Hence, we beg the grieving Mother to enable us to share her sufferings. One way we can do this is to bring love and comfort to others in their distress. Another way is to offer up all our own sufferings to be united with those of Mary and her Son.

TO CHRIST THROUGH MARY (7-8)

In the seventh and eighth couplets the poet asks Mary to lead us to Christ — thus expressing the classic theme of going to Christ through his Mother.

First we once more ask to grieve with Mary, weeping and mourning for Christ in the knowledge of what he has done for us. This knowledgeable grief should lead us to prayer, in which we also call upon Mary to aid us.

Inevitably this co-suffering will lead us to bear Christ's death in us — death to sin and ultimately death to this world.

Because of our weakness none of this is possible by our own efforts. We need the grace of God through Mary's example and intercession, for, as John Paul II has indicated, she offered us a unique contribution to the Gospel of suffering:

"As a witness to her Son's Passion by her *presence*, and as a sharer in it by her *compassion*, Mary offered a unique contribution to the Gospel of suffering, by embodying in anticipation the expression of St. Paul which was quoted above [cf. Colossians 1:24]. She truly has a special title to be able to claim that she 'completes in her flesh' — as already in her heart — 'what is lacking in Christ's afflictions'" (John Paul II: Apostolic Letter *On the Christian Meaning of Human Suffering*, no. 25).

PLEA FOR MARY'S HELP (9-10)

The last two couplets form a plea for help — to Mary herself and then to Christ. The faithful ask Mary to ensure that their sufferings will unite with Christ even in death. They then beg Christ to have Mary defend them in their time of death so that they may attain victory through his Cross.

Although the poem does not say it, Mary's aid is forthcoming only because Christ from the Cross commends her to us and us to her — as Leo XIII so well states: "Behold your son... Behold your Mother" (John 19:26-27), are seen by the Church as a special parting gift, by which Christ the Lord "entrusted" to his Mother "all his disciples as her children" (Encyclical Letter *The Month of October*) and entrusted his Mother to his disciples to be honored and revered.

This act of commending or entrusting is part of the Mystery of Christ's Passion and Mary's co-suffering. The Liturgy refers to the Blessed Virgin as one who stood by the Cross and tenderly looked on the wounds of her Son, whose death she knew would redeem the world. It places on her lips the words of the Apostle: "I endure all for the sake of the Elect, so that they too may achieve salvation in Christ Jesus with eternal glory" (2 Timothy 2:10).

In the person of John, our Lord made all his disciples living signs of his own love for his Mother: they receive her as a precious inheritance from their Master, and in heeding what she says they conscientiously keep the words of their Master.

"Mary's Motherhood that becomes man's inheritance is a gift: a gift that Christ himself makes personally to every individual. The Redeemer entrusts Mary to John because he entrusts John to Mary. At the foot of the Cross there begins that special entrusting of humanity to the Mother of Christ which in the history of the Church has been practiced and expressed in different ways.... Entrusting is the response to a person's love, and in particular to the love of a mother....

"Thus the Christian seeks to be taken into that maternal charity with which the Redeemer's Mother 'cares for the brethren of her Son' (*Constitution on the Church*, no. 62) 'in whose birth and development she cooperates' (*Ibid.*, no. 63) in the measure of the gift proper to each one through the power of Christ's Spirit" (John Paul II: Encyclical Letter *Mother of the Redeemer*, no. 45).

Thus, the poem hints at the infinite goodness of God who does not abandon those who stray from him but in marvelous ways calls them back to him. He gave the Blessed Virgin Mary, sinless as she was, a heart of compassion for sinners.

Seeing her love as our Mother, we readily turn to her with trust as we ask God's forgiveness. Seeing her beauty of spirit, we naturally seek to turn away from sin in its ugliness. Taking to heart her words and example, we truly learn to keep the commandments of God's Son until we are "safe in heaven eternally."

10

The Memorare

A BEAUTIFUL AND POPULAR PRAYER

One of the most beautiful and popular of all prayers to Mary is the *Memorare* (mem-awr-RAH-ray), so called after its first word in Latin — which means "remember." There are a host of English translations, each with its own special slant and its own adherents.

Perhaps the most known is the one that appeared in the 1969 English edition of the *Enchiridion of Indulgences*:

> *Remember, O most gracious Virgin Mary,*
> *that never was it known*
> *that anyone who fled to your protection,*
> *implored your help and sought your intercession,*
> *was left unaided.*
>
> *Inspired with this confidence,*
> *I fly to you, O Virgin of Virgins, my Mother;*
> *to you do I come,*
> *before you I stand, sinful and sorrowful.*
> *O Mother of the Word Incarnate,*

despise not my petitions,
but in your mercy hear and answer me.

ORIGIN OF THE PRAYER

The *Memorare* was long attributed to St. Bernard of Clairvaux (1090-1153), but modern scholars have ascertained that this is not the case. They believe it comes from a longer *Memorare* used by the Eastern Church dating from the eighth to the tenth centuries. The Latin version of the prayer appeared in the eleventh century and was popularized by a French priest devoted to the poor, Claude Bernard, who died in 1641.

Although St. Bernard may not have composed this beautiful prayer, he certainly laid the groundwork for its acceptance. His works are filled with the sentiments on which the prayer is based.

The sermons about our Lady preached by this peerless devotee of the Virgin are famous and so are his Marian catch phrases: "Of Mary there is never enough"; "Look at the Star, call upon Mary"; "Let no one speak a word about your compassion if even one of those who invoked you in need can remember that your compassion was not given."

The most celebrated example of the power of the *Memorare* was the case of Alphonsus Ratisbon, who as a non-Christian was challenged to recite it. He did so and was later converted to the Catholic Faith (January 20, 1842) after seeing a vision of the Blessed Virgin. He went on to co-found two religious congregations (Congregation of Sion and Fathers of Sion).

Another heralded example was that of St. Francis de Sales. As a seventeen-year-old student studying in Paris, Francis encountered a dryness of soul that led him to believe that all he did for love of God was of no avail for he was already damned.

Francis lost his appetite, was tormented by lack of sleep, and became so despondent that he incurred the pity of all who encountered him. One evening he chanced to enter a church in which he found a plaque with the *Memorare* on it.

Kneeling before the altar, he devoutly recited the prayer, renewed the consecration of his virginity to Mary that he had made previously, and promised to recite the Rosary daily. After adding a short prayer of his own to our Lady, Francis was overjoyed to see his despondency lift.

Our Blessed Mother had regained for him inner peace as well as physical restoration. For the remainder of his life, Francis continued to be devoted to Mary, writing books and preaching sermons in her honor. He even wrote a longer version of the *Memorare* (see below).

MARIAN TITLES AND TEACHING

The *Memorare* contains two beautiful titles of Mary. She is the "most gracious Virgin Mary" — not only "gracious" meaning grace-laden, grace-filled, but a Virgin.

Indeed, Mary is the "Virgin of Virgins" but at the same time our "Mother," the Mother of all human beings. Finally, she is also the Mother of the Word Incarnate — that is, she is the Mother of the second Person of the Blessed Trinity, the Mother of God.

We could say that much of the teaching of the Church about our Lady can be found in these brief phrases. For example, we can find in it: the Immaculate Conception ("gracious," grace-filled), the Virgin Birth ("Virgin of Virgins"), the Divine Motherhood ("Mother of the Word Incarnate"), Mary's Spiritual Motherhood ("my Mother"), and the Mediation of Mary ("hear and answer me").

The underlying teaching of this prayer can be taken from St. Bernard's sermon entitled, "The Aqueduct." At the very beginning Mary received from God the principal fullness of grace, which is Jesus Christ, in order to share him with us.

She also received a second fullness, which is the result of the first, the fullness of the graces that we receive through her prayers. Hence, we should invoke her with the greatest of confidence.

St. Bernard assures us that if Mary prays for us, we shall be saved. Just as the Father cannot help but hear the Son, so the Son cannot help but hear his Mother.

MARIAN SENTIMENTS

The *Memorare* is popular with devoted clients of our Lady because of its simple yet eloquent fervor. Every line breathes a sincere and deep *love for Mary* as our Heavenly Mother.

It is buttressed on sentiments like those voiced by St. John Berchmans: "O most sweet Lady, happy are those who love you. If I love Mary, I am certain of final perseverance and I shall obtain whatever I ask from God."

The *Memorare* also exudes a *staunch and unwavering hope in Mary's powerful intercession* with God: never was it known that anyone who called upon Mary was left *unaided*. No ifs, ands, or buts. *Call on Mary and be helped.*

Underlying these sentiments are those expressed in the noted prayer of St. Bernard reproduced in the Introduction, pp. 4-5, and in the following excerpt from his *Homily 7 on Mary*:

"Our Queen has gone before us, and so glorious has been her entry into paradise that we, her servants, confidently ask our Mistress, calling out: 'Draw us after you and we shall run in the fragrance of your perfumes' (Song of Songs 1:3). As the Mother of our Judge and the Mother of Mercy, she will humbly and efficaciously handle the affairs of our salvation.

"Earth has sent a priceless gift up to heaven, so that by giving and receiving within the blessed bond of friendship, the human is wedded to the Divine, earth to heaven, the depths to the heights. A

sublime fruit of the earth has gone up to heaven, from which alone descend the best gifts, the perfect gifts.

"The Blessed Virgin has ascended on high, and therefore she too will give gifts to human beings. And why not? Surely neither the ability nor the will to do so is lacking to her. She is the Queen of heaven; she is compassionate; finally, she is the Mother of the only-begotten Son of God.

"And nothing can so commend the greatness of her power or her love unless perhaps we do not believe that the Son of God honors his Mother, or unless we doubt Mary's Maternity (which means that Love itself that is born of God rested within her physically for nine months) evoked a response of love in her heart.

"But this I say for our benefit, knowing that perfect charity which seeks not its own is not easily found in the midst of our great misery."

Finally, an aura of *spiritual peace* lies beneath the words of the *Memorare*. "Sinful and sorrowful," the pray-er stands before the Mother of God, with a fearful heart but with the sure knowledge of being heard and forgiven. The supplicant has done what God wanted. It is now Mary's task to do what the supplicant asks. And in the natural line of things, she will do what she is asked.

This sentiment is founded on the belief that Mary is so merciful and kind that when people come to her and recommend themselves to her, she does not question their merits or whether they are worthy or unworthy to receive her attention. She simply hears and helps everybody who comes to her.

OTHER *MEMORARES*

The *Memorare* has become most popular with clients of Mary. In fact, it spawned not only similar prayers to other Saints, for example to St. Joseph and St. Anthony, but also other *Memorares* to our Lady.

The *Memorares* to other Saints read very much like the one to our Lady. The only change is in the name of the person addressed.

The other *Memorares* to Mary use the thoughts of the original prayer but in one case set them in a poetic version and in another arrange them in a much longer version.

The poetic version was written by St. Louis de Montfort:

> Remember, O Virgin above,
> Whose heart is wholly free from stain,
> That it has never been heard of
> For prayer to you to be in vain.
>
> No one with total confidence
> Ever asked of you a favor
> Without receiving assistance
> And experiencing your sweet savor.
>
> With a contrite heart, O Mary,
> Your holy Name I dare invoke
> And present a poor sinner's plea
> For protection under your cloak
>
> Show forth your August clemency
> By obtaining from your dear Son
> Repentance and pardon for me
> Of all the sins I may have done.
>
> Look on your servant with kindness;
> Do not send me away empty.
> For your renowned love and goodness
> Are greater than my sins can be.

The *Memorare* of St. Francis de Sales is also worth quoting because of the nuanced themes it introduces:

> Most holy Virgin, remember that you are my Mother and I am your child. . ., that you are most powerful and I am very weak. I beg you, dear Mother, to guide and defend me in all my ways and actions.

Gracious Virgin, do not tell me that you cannot do so. For your beloved Son has given you all power! Do not tell me that you should not do so. For you are the common Mother of all human beings and singularly mine....

If you were unable to do so, I would excuse it with the words: "It is true that she is my Mother and loves me like her child but the poor thing lacks power to do so."

If you were not my Mother, I would rightly say with patience: "She is indeed rich enough to assist me; however since she is not my Mother, she does not love me....

Therefore, most holy Virgin, since you are my Mother and also are so powerful, how can I excuse you if you do not comfort me and grant me your assistance?

You see then, dear Mother, that you are obliged to grant all my requests.

For the honor and glory of your Son, accept me as your child, without regard for my wretchedness and my sins. Deliver my soul and body from all evil and grant me all your virtues, especially humility!

Finally, bestow upon me all the gifts, goods, and graces that are pleasing to the Blessed Trinity, Father, Son, and Holy Spirit.

No matter which *Memorare* we make use of, and even if we do not utilize its words, we are assured of having Mary's aid so long as we approach her with the sentiments of the prayer. For then our Lady will ensure that our requests will be granted and we will once again go *to Jesus through Mary*.

11

The Litany of Loreto

LITANY — A SPECIAL FORM OF PRAYER

After the *Hail Mary*, the Litany of Loreto is perhaps the most popular prayer in honor of Mary known to Catholic piety. At the same time, it is probably the second most well-known Litany in the Church (after the Litany of the Saints).

Once these constituted the only two Litanies permitted for public recitation in the Western Church. Now there are six others: the Litanies of the Holy Name, the Sacred Heart, the Precious Blood, St. Joseph, the Dying, and the newest one — the Litany of the Blessed Virgin Mary found in the *Order of Crowning an Image of the Blessed Virgin Mary*, approved in 1981 (English translation published in 1986).

The word Litany designates a prayer formed by a series of brief invocations or supplications to which the assembly responds with a short refrain. It is known as an excellent type of prayer, simple and clear — at one and the same time supplication and instruction.

The earliest form of the Litany is found in the Bible in Psalm 136. Each half-verse of the psalm is followed by a refrain: "Give thanks to the Lord... *for his mercy endures forever.*"

Scholars find other traces of Litanies in the First Letter to Timothy (2:1-3), the writings known as the Apostolic Fathers, and the early Christian writer Lactantius, among others.

Hence, it is little wonder that when the early Church celebrated the Eucharist, she made use of Litany-like prayers in the Prayer of the Faithful. In time, this fell into disuse, and the only Litany-form prayers in the Mass were the *Kyrie* (Lord, have mercy) and *Agnus Dei* (Lamb of God) — both truncated Litanies.

Side by side with these Litanies of *supplication* there were Litanies of *invocation*. The earliest testimony of collective invocation of the inhabitants of heaven is found in a Greek text from Asia Minor around the year 400.

By the seventh century, there was the Litany of the Saints, which spread far and wide through the efforts of missionary Irish monks. It was not a series of praises but a series of invocations and then supplications. Such prayer formularies had a popular character and were used in processions, at occasions of penance, on the Easter Vigil, at ordinations, and for the dying.

Later, the so-called *Greater Litanies* were used on April 25 to counteract a pagan fertility feast. And on the Monday, Tuesday, and Wednesday before the Solemnity of the Ascension, the Church celebrated the *Minor Litanies* to pray for deliverance from earthquakes and other natural disasters.

These Litanies were accompanied by religious processions and pageantry that appealed to many of the people. Hence, they spawned a host of other Litanies. Scholars tell us that by 1601, there were at least sixty Litanies in public use.

Gradually, most of the Litanies were eliminated by the Church because they were seen as deviations. The only two retained for public use were the Litany of the Saints and the Litany of Loreto. In time, the other official Litanies mentioned above came into play.

In our day, the Litany prayer-form has made a comeback. We have Litany-type prayers in the new Mass and new Office. In the former there are the Responsorial Psalm and Prayer of the Faithful; in the latter there are the Intercessions.

Origin of the Litany of Loreto

The magnificent series of invocations in honor of our Lady that comprises the Litany of Loreto is doubtless the work of many hands. Its formulas are somewhat mysterious but intelligible to those possessed of a Christian culture, forming a prayer of exquisite charm. Such a prayer constructs salutation and supplication out of the glorious titles of the Blessed Virgin and at the same time details all the reasons for our confidence in her.

Some of the Litany's invocations are deeply poetic and richly symbolic while others are simpler and charged with poignant hope. Still others bring forth a royal pageantry for the cortege of the faithful.

The origin of the Litany is shrouded in mystery. We have no knowledge of its author. Neither do we know how or why it was adopted into the cultic practice of the Shrine of the Holy House of Loreto (whence its name). This was the House in which legend says the Blessed Mother received the Angel's Annunciation.

This House was said to have been transferred by "Angels" (a word now believed to refer to Crusaders) from Nazareth to Dalmatia in 1291 and ultimately to Loreto in east central Italy (near the Adriatic Sea) in 1294. From that time, it has become one of the most famous shrines of our Lady in the world.

The final compiler of the Litany put together the fruit of positive and negative experiences of three centuries' pastoral usage at the Shrine. In his work, he was inspired by various Marian Litanies in use at the time, but he also had in mind the model of all Litany-forms — the majestic Litany of the Saints.

In the Litany of the Saints, Mary heads the list of Saints and is invoked three times: *Holy Mary, pray for us; Holy Mother of God, pray for us; Holy Virgin of virgins, pray for us.* These invocations — together with the introductory series of invocations to the Trinity — are retained in her own Litany.

There seems little doubt that the Litany of Loreto dates from between 1150 and 1200 and probably originated at Paris or its environs.

The final author composed a Litany text that was briefer than other texts already existing (by notably reducing the number of invocations), more smooth (by avoiding overly complex invocations), more organized in the arrangement of the material, and more balanced in content.

The Litany was also sufficiently Biblical and patristic in tone, rooted in poetic and theological sources so as to satisfy aesthetic and doctrinal demands, and devoid of extravagant invocations.

The list of praises to our Lady (51 titles in all) owes much to prayers of the Greek Church — in particular the Akathist Hymn (translated into Latin and first published about 800 at Venice). It is also based on the writings of the Fathers of the first six centuries.

Originally, the Litany also included fifteen more invocations. Some of them were: Our Lady of Humility, Mother of Mercy, Temple of the Spirit, Gate of Redemption, and Queen of Disciples.

From 1587 onward, the Popes took control of the Litany of Loreto. They exercised vigilant care over this simple and expressive prayer in order to keep its recitation alive, its formulas clear, and its contents relevant. In 1631, 1821, and 1839, the Sacred Congregation of Rites prohibited the addition of any invocations to the Litany without the explicit authorization of the Apostolic See.

MODERN ADDITIONS TO THE LITANY

At the same time however, many dioceses, religious families, and shrines received authorization to insert one or at most two invocations that had to do with the particular Marian title or aspect proper to them. Such invocations had to be simple and in accord with the structural and thematic balance of the formulary.

In the nineteenth and twentieth centuries, the Popes themselves have added a few significant invocations to the Litany. Indeed it seems that the Litany has become the customary place for modern Pontiffs to leave vibrant memorials of their Marian devotion.

After the solemn definition of the Immaculate Conception on December 8, 1854, the invocation "Queen conceived without original sin" was added by the nature of things and as a result of a universal spontaneous initiative rather than by Apostolic indult.

Leo XIII inserted two invocations. In 1883, the "Pope of the Encyclical on the Rosary" almost naturally added the invocation "Queen of the Most Holy Rosary." In 1903, he inserted the invocation "Mother of Good Counsel" in homage to the piety of his native land, which housed the Sanctuary of the Mother of Good Counsel at Genzano.

In 1916, during the First World War, Benedict XV added the invocation "Queen of Peace" to pray for the end of the raging conflict.

Finally, in 1951, Pius XII introduced the invocation "Queen assumed into heaven" as a follow-up to the dogmatic definition of the Assumption of Mary body and soul into heaven, which he had decreed in 1950.

"Mother of the Church"

In keeping with this tradition, the present Holy Father, John Paul II, in 1980 announced the insertion of a new invocation in this Litany: "Mother of the Church." In doing so, he was pursuing the dialogue between the Apostolic See and the Local Churches with respect to this Litany and was also including therein a perpetual reminder of the greatest event of our age — the celebration of the Second Vatican Council.

However, in this case, the Pope did not obligate anyone to use the new invocation. He granted a concession for its use to any Episcopal Conference that would take advantage of it. In essence, this concession was the consequence of the Marian piety of the last three Popes as well as the people.

The title "Mother of the Church" was announced by Pope Paul VI during the Council. The proclamation came after the promulgation of the *Constitution on the Church*, November 21, 1964. The Pope chose the occasion to give Mary a title that "expresses with wonderful brevity the exalted place in the Church that the Church recognizes as proper to the Mother of God."

Since that time, this title has been taken to heart by the People of God. There have been churches dedicated to Mary under that title, centers of study and social activities placed under its protection, religious congregations and pious associations assigned to its patronage, and publications bearing its name.

Above all, the 1975 second edition of the revised *Roman Missal* included a Votive Mass of Mary, Mother of the Church. This title has become part of the Church's Liturgy and spiritual life.

This new optional invocation sums up the spiritual motherhood that the Mother of Jesus exercises toward the members of his Mystical Body, the Church, of which Christ is the Head.

It is intended to call attention to the Council's teaching about the true beauty of the face of the Church, Spouse of Christ, and our teacher and mother as well as about Mary's role in the Mystery of Christ and his Church.

The reason why Mary is Mother of the Church is that she is Mother of God and Associate of Christ in his saving work. She remained joined to her Son's saving work in the new economy in which he freed human beings from sin by the Mysteries of his flesh.

On Calvary, Jesus gave John into Mary's care. Since John represented humanity, this designated Mary Mother of the Human Race. At the Annunciation, Mary conceived Christ by the Spirit's power. After Christ's Resurrection, she prayed with the disciples for the Spirit's coming in order that the Church, her Son's Body, might be born on Pentecost.

Through her faith and love, Mary's Maternity reached out to all the members of Jesus' Mystical Body.

Mary is also Mother of the Church because she is the model of virtues. As Pope Paul VI stated: "Jesus gave us Mary as our Mother and proposed her as a Model to be imitated."

"QUEEN OF FAMILIES"

On December 31, 1995, the Congregation for Divine Worship and the Discipline of the Sacraments informed the Episcopal Conferences of the world that Pope John Paul II empowered them to insert the invocation "Queen of families" after "Queen of the most holy Rosary" and before "Queen of peace."

This new invocation flows naturally from the fact that Mary is Mother of the Church. She is also Mother of the Domestic Church — the family.

In his 1981 Apostolic Exhortation *The Christian Family in the Modern World* (*Familiaris Consortio*), John Paul II stated: "May Christ the Lord, the Universal King, the *King of Families*, be present in every Christian home as he was at Cana, bestowing light, joy, serenity, and strength."

By the side of the *King of Families* there shines forth the *Queen of Families*. And it is the Pope himself who sets forth the meaning of this new invocation:

"Mary called herself the '*Handmaid of the Lord*' (Luke 1:38). Through obedience to the Word of God she accepted her lofty, yet not easy vocation as wife and mother in the family of Nazareth. Putting herself at God's service, she also put herself at the service of others: a service of love.

"Precisely through this service Mary was able to experience in her life a mysterious but authentic 'reign.' It is not by chance that she is invoked as 'Queen of heaven and earth.' The entire community of believers thus invokes her; many nations and peoples call upon her as their 'Queen.' For her 'to reign' is to serve! Her service is 'to reign.'

"This is the way in which authority needs to be understood both in the family and in society and in the Church.... The maternal 'reign' of Mary consists in this. She who was, in all her being, a gift for her Son has also become a gift for the sons and daughters of the whole human race, awakening profound trust in those who seek her guidance along the difficult paths of life on the way to their definitive and transcendental destiny" (*Letter to Women*, June 29, 1995).

CONTENTS OF THE LITANY

The Litany opens with the familiar three invocations: *Lord, have mercy; Christ, have mercy; Lord, have mercy.* Then follow the four invocations to the individual Divine Persons and the Trinity as a whole, asking for mercy: *God the Father of heaven; God the Son, Redeemer of the world; God the Holy Spirit; and Holy Trinity, One God.*

The actual Litany invoking Mary's prayers now begins. The first twenty invocations (twenty-one with *Mother of the Church*) are Marian praises addressed to Mary as *Holy; Mother;* and *Virgin.*

Holy Mary
Holy Mother of God
Holy Virgin of virgins
Mother of Christ
Mother of the Church
Mother of Divine Grace
Mother most pure
Mother most chaste
Mother inviolate

Mother undefiled
Mother most amiable
Mother most admirable
Mother of good counsel
Mother of our Creator
Mother of our Savior
Virgin most prudent
Virgin most venerable
Virgin most renowned

Virgin most powerful   *Virgin most faithful*
Virgin most merciful

The next thirteen invocations are remarkable descriptions of our Lady's *office*, *power*, and *virtues*.

Mirror of justice   *Mystical rose*
Seat of wisdom   *Tower of David*
Cause of our joy   *Tower of ivory*
Spiritual vessel   *House of gold*
Vessel of honor   *Ark of the covenant*
Singular vessel of   *Gate of heaven*
   devotion *Morning star*

These are followed by four *common* titles.

Health of the sick   *Comforter of the afflicted*
Refuge of sinners   *Help of Christians*

Thirteen titles go on to address Mary as *Queen* of the Communion of Saints.

Queen of Angels   *Queen of all Saints*
Queen of Patriarchs   *Queen conceived without*
Queen of Prophets   *original sin*
Queen of Apostles   *Queen assumed into heaven*
Queen of Martyrs   *Queen of the most holy Rosary*
Queen of Confessors   *Queen of families*
Queen of Virgins   *Queen of peace*

The Litany proper comes to an end with the traditional *Lamb of God* invocations followed by the versicle and response:

V.   *Pray for us, O holy Mother of God.*
R.   *That we may be worthy of the promises of Christ.*

Then the Litany concludes with the Opening Prayer from the Common of the Blessed Virgin Mary:

Let us pray. Grant, we beseech you, O Lord God, that we your servants may enjoy lasting health of mind and body, and by the glorious intercession of the Blessed Mary, ever Virgin, be delivered from present sorrow and enter into the joy of eternal happiness. Through Christ our Lord.

BENEFICIAL EFFECTS

Down through the centuries, the Litany of Loreto has always remained a simple yet powerful prayer in honor of our Lady. It has enabled Mary's clients to honor her by the alternation of admiring contemplation and confident supplication found in each title.

At the same time, the Litany has had many beneficial effects on the People of God. Its invocations are rich in doctrine, adding up to a quasi-synthesis of Catholic teaching about Mary.

As Catholics repeat the praise of the one they view as a powerful Mediatrix with her Son, they grow in knowledge and love of their heavenly Mother through the beauty and power of this time-tested prayer.

The Litany has also provided much inspiration for countless artists who have interpreted the invocations according to their personal inclinations. Hence, the themes of these invocations have been painted, set to music, and even engraved.

Indeed, some have claimed that the Litany is the most famous prayer to Mary — although others more logically point to the Hail Mary. Whether it is first or second on the Marian prayer-scale, the Litany of Loreto is a wonderful instrument for going *to Jesus through Mary!*

12

The Litany of the Blessed Virgin Mary

A New Litany of Mary

On March 25, 1981, the Church issued a new Litany in honor of Mary. It formed part of the *Order of Crowning an Image of the Blessed Virgin Mary*, whose official English translation appeared in 1987 in the United States.

In this way, the Church reiterated that the best way to honor the Mother of God is through the Liturgy. And she also presented us with a more modern rendition of her Marian teaching.

The new rite speaks the language of people today yet is steeped in the tradition of the Church. The prayers are especially eloquent and based on optimum sources: (1) God's living Word in the Bible; (2) Vatican II's pastoral orientation and emphasis in contemporary Catholic culture; and (3) the Church's monumental treasury of liturgical texts.

A key theme is the relationship of Mary's Queenship and her participation in the Paschal Mystery. Another is how to understand that Queenship — in the Gospel sense of love and service. The rite aims to inspire all who take part in it to make a more fervent commitment to the Christian life — while utilizing terms and themes that are relevant and comprehensible in our day.

From Lowliness to Glory

The new Litany provides a Biblical basis for Christ's Kingship and Mary's Queenship and roots them both in the Paschal Mystery: Christ's Passion and Resurrection-Ascension.

An integral part of the Divine plan of salvation was that Christ's abasement should be followed by his exaltation at the right hand of the Father. This abasement-exaltation (Paschal Mystery) is prolonged in the members of the Mystical Body of Christ, especially Mary, his *Mother* and *perfect follower*.

For example, Mary termed herself the *Handmaid of the Lord*. She was chosen as the *Mother of the Redeemer* (translated as "Lord" in the official text) and the real *Mother of all the living*. She now reigns in glory with her Son above the choirs of Angels. And she offers prayers for all human beings as the *Advocate of grace* and *Queen of mercy*.

Recitation of this Litany unquestionably leads people to live in the light of the Paschal Mystery. It does so by urging all to deny themselves and "lose" their lives in order to gain the souls of their brothers and sisters on earth. By following the lowly things of this world they will reach the heights of the other world.

In essence, the Litany inspires us to emulate Mary's lowly life, which was itself an imitation of Christ's life.

Although it shows us Mary crowned Queen of heaven, it also reminds us of the unpretentious nature of her life on earth.

Mary's home in Nazareth was a modest one. Her lowly life was lived in close relation with God the Father through the power of the Holy Spirit and in loving union with the Word who became flesh in her at the moment of her declaration of servanthood (cf. Luke 1:38).

Immediately after that event, Mary departed to help her cousin Elizabeth who dwelt in the hill country at a town of Judah (cf. Luke 1:39). Still travel-logged, Mary nonetheless gave voice to her famous *Magnificat* — a song of praise to the Lord for all his works. Among other things, it sets forth the spirituality of the "Poor of Yahweh," God's lowly righteous ones who suffer abasement on earth.

During our Lord's Infancy and Public Life, Mary was always unobtrusive. She lived with the constant memory of Simeon's prediction of the sorrow that would be hers (cf. Luke 2:35).

At Cana, while requesting help for a wedding couple, she glimpsed the fact that her Son had a timetable to adhere to for his life work. Then, all the while Jesus journeyed through the Promised Land, she meditated on his Word in obscurity (cf. Luke 11:28).

Finally, Mary stood courageously beneath the Cross on Calvary. This was the ultimate abasement of her Son as he drew all things to himself (cf. John 12:32).

A QUEENSHIP OF LOVE AND SPIRIT

On earth, then, Mary was God's poor and lowly Handmaid, who kept his Word. Now he has exalted her as Queen in heaven. The same fate awaits all those who in our day are persecuted and humiliated because of their faithfulness to the Gospel.

However, this Queenship is not one of power and possessions but one of *love and service*, just as is the Kingship of Christ: "My kingdom does not belong to this world" (John 18:16); "The Son of Man has come not to be served by others but to serve, to give his life as a ransom for the many" (Matthew 20:28).

On earth Mary was the consummate Handmaid of the Lord, ever humble and self-effacing. She dedicated herself completely to her Son and his work. Following his lead, she served the Mystery of the Redemption in close union with him.

Assumed gloriously into heaven, she is a *minister of holiness*, continuing to manifest this love and service. She intercedes with God for the salvation of all her children.

In a similar manner, all who imitate Christ by emulating Mary on earth will reign with Christ in heaven, in accord with the words of St. Paul: "If we have died with him we shall also rise with him; if we persevere we shall also reign with him" (2 Timothy 2:11).

Thus, the path to this royalty is no different for us than it was for the Queenship of Mary. It entails *love and service*.

THE REAL MEANING OF MARY'S QUEENSHIP

Like the whole Rite, the Litany pinpoints the four major qualities that make Mary a Queen. She is (1) the *Mother* of the Son of God and Messianic King; (2) the loving *Associate* (or *Helper*) *of the Redeemer*; (3) the *perfect follower* (or *Disciple*) *of Christ*; and (4) the most excellent member of the Church.

(1) Mary is Queen because she is *Mother of the Word Incarnate*. She brought forth a Son who at the very moment of his conception was King and Lord of all things — even as man. In this Word "were created all things in heaven and on earth, the visible and the invisible, whether thrones or dominations or principalities or powers; all things were created through him and for him" (Colossians 1:16).

Mary is Queen also because she is the *Mother of the Messianic King*. She bore a Son about whom the Angel said:

"He will be great and will be called Son of the Most High, and the Lord God will give him the throne of David his father, and he will rule over the house of Jacob forever, and of his kingdom there will be no end" (Luke 1:32-33).

(2) Mary is Queen because she was *associated wholeheartedly with Christ the Redeemer*. By an eternal plan of God, the Blessed Virgin is the new Eve, and she played a great part in the work of salvation by which Jesus, the new Adam, redeemed us and purchased us for him-

self not with corruptible gold or silver but with his Precious Blood
(cf. I Peter 1:18-19) and made us into a kingdom for our God (cf.
Revelation 5:10).

(3) Mary is Queen because she was the *perfect disciple of Christ.*
This is a new theme stressed by Vatican II while citing the words
of the Book of Revelation: "Remain faithful until death, and I will
give you the crown of life.... I will give the victor the right to sit
with me on my throne, as I myself first won the victory and sit with
my father on his throne" (Revelation 2:10; 3:21).

In numbers 55-59 of the *Constitution on the Church,* Vatican II
spelled out the role of the Blessed Virgin in the economy of salvation. The conciliar text makes it clear that Mary was totally united
with her Son "in the work of salvation... from the time of Christ's
virginal conception to his death."

The rite incorporates this theme in a concise and concrete fashion: "Mary consented to the Divine Plan and advanced in the journey of faith. She heard and kept the Word of God and faithfully
preserved her union with the Son even to the Cross. She then persevered in prayer together with the Church and became proficient in
the love of God."

(4) Mary is Queen because she is the *untarnished image of the Church*
or, as the Council put it, "the most excellent member of the Church."
She is "blessed among women" (Luke 1:42) and holds a preeminent place in the Communion of Saints for a twofold reason: her
mission and her holiness.

Mary stands out in the chosen race, priestly people, and holy
nation that is the Church because of the singular mission given her
with respect to the Church and all members of Christ's Mystical
Body, and because of her copious virtues and fullness of grace. Therefore, she deserves to be called the "Lady" of human beings and
Angels, and the "Queen" of all Saints.

Indeed, Mary's glory reverberates even outside the daughter
of Adam and our Lady. She is thus not only the Joy of Israel and
the Splendor of the Church but also the Pride of the human race!

INVOCATIONS RELEVANT TO OUR DAY

A brief overview of the invocations found in the Litany will quickly show how relevant they are to our day. It should move all of us to make use of this beautiful prayer to our Lady.

Some of these invocations are already familiar to us: the three-fold invocation of the Trinity beginning with *Lord, have mercy*; the beloved response after the Marian invocations: *pray for us*; the first three invocations to our Lady: *Holy Mary; Holy Mother of God; Holy Virgin of virgins* (although the official English translation renders it as *Most honored of virgins*); and the threefold invocation to the *Lamb of God* at the end.

Other invocations of the Litany place the area of Mary's Queenship in greater perspective. Mary is *Queen of love*, that is, she is preeminent in Christian charity, and she leads all the followers of Christ to attain charity. At the same time, she is also *Queen of mercy* and *Queen of peace*, for mercy and peace result from charity.

Also enumerated are the groups that make up Mary's kingdom and experience the depth of her service and the purity of her love. They are angelical, Old Testament, and New Testament groups: *angels, patriarchs, prophets, apostles, martyrs, confessors, virgins*, and *all saints*.

Finally, the Litany likens the boundaries of Mary's kingdom to those of her Son's. She is Queen of *the world*, of *heaven*, and of *the universe*.

The composers of this splendid Litany drew invocations from the finest sources of the Church. Sacred Scripture yielded *Virgin daughter of Zion; Handmaid of the Lord; Full of grace; Woman clothed with the sun; Woman crowned with the stars*; and *Joy of Israel*.

Previous Litanies provided the first three invocations and the final threefold invocation of *Lamb of God* (Litany of the Saints) and the group of invocations from *Queen of angels* to *Queen conceived without original sin* (Litany of Loreto).

The Documents of Vatican II are also represented by invocations: *Finest fruit of the redemption*; *Queen of the universe*; and *Helper of the Redeemer*.

Finally, four invocations come from the Church's liturgical texts: *Advocate of grace* (Preface for the Immaculate Conception); *Queen of heaven*; *Queen of the world*; and *Queen of mercy*.

Even this cursory look at the new Litany shows the riches that it contains. By making use of its invocations, we can partake of these riches and reach the heavenly kingdom — going *to Jesus through Mary*. This is what the concluding prayer of the Litany wishes for us all.

THE NEW LITANY

Lord, have mercy.   *Lord, have mercy.*
Christ, have mercy.   *Christ, have mercy.*
Lord, have mercy.   *Lord, have mercy.*

God, our Father in heaven, have mercy on us.
God, the Son, Redeemer of the world, have mercy on us.
God, the Holy Spirit, have mercy on us.
Holy Trinity, one God, have mercy on us.

Holy Mary, pray for us (repeated after each invocation)
Holy Mother of God
Most honored of virgins

Chosen daughter of the Father
Mother of Christ the King
Glory of the Holy Spirit

Virgin daughter of Zion
Virgin poor and humble
Virgin gentle and obedient

Handmaid of the Lord
Mother of the Lord
Helper of the Redeemer

Full of grace
Fountain of beauty
Model of virtue

Finest fruit of the redemption
Perfect disciple of Christ
Untarnished image of the Church

Woman transformed
Woman clothed with the sun
Woman crowned with stars

Gentle Lady
Gracious Lady
Our Lady

Joy of Israel
Splendor of the Church
Pride of the human race

Advocate of grace
Minister of holiness
Champion of God's people

Queen of love
Queen of mercy
Queen of peace

Queen of angels
Queen of patriarchs and prophets
Queen of apostles and martyrs
Queen of confessors and virgins
Queen of all saints
Queen conceived without original sin

Queen assumed into heaven

Queen of all the earth
Queen of heaven
Queen of the universe

Lamb of God, you take away the sins of the world;
spare us, O Lord.
Lamb of God, you take away the sins of the world;
hear us, O Lord.
Lamb of God, you take away the sins of the world;
have mercy on us.

Pray for us, O glorious Mother of the Lord.
That we may become worthy of the promises of Christ.

God of mercy,
listen to the prayers of your servants
who have honored your handmaid Mary as mother and Queen.
Grant that by your grace
we may serve you and our neighbor on earth
and be welcomed into your eternal kingdom.

We ask this through Christ our Lord.

Appendix

SIXTY CLASSIC PRAYERS OF CATHOLICS TO MARY

In addition to the traditional quasi-official prayers of the Church to Mary there are classic prayers of Catholics to our Lady. Of these the following sixty are among the best known and deserve to be reprinted in a book of Marian prayers.

1. Mary, Mother of the Savior of the World

This prayer, found in Egypt, was chiseled by an anonymous hand on a terracotta around the third or fourth century. The text is inspired by the Angel's salutation to Mary.

O immaculate virgin, Mother of God, full of grace, the one whom you brought forth, Emmanuel, is the fruit of your womb. In your Motherhood you have nurtured all human beings. You surpass all praise and all glory.

I salute you, Mother of God, joy of the Angels, because you surpass in fullness what the Prophets have said about you. The Lord is with you: you gave life to the Savior of the world.

2. Mary, Vessel of God's Mysteries

In this short beautiful prayer, St. Gregory the Wonderworker (d. 270) pinpoints the idea that Mary knows all the Divine Mysteries and participated in most of them.

Mary, you are the vessel and tabernacle containing all Mysteries. You know what the Patriarchs did not know; you experienced what was not revealed to the Angels; you heard what the Prophets did not hear. In short, everything that was hidden from preceding generations was made known to you; even more, most of these wonders depended on you.

3. Mary, Our Hope

In this prayer, St. Ephrem of Edessa (d. 373) calls Mary the hope for all hopeless and sinful human beings and implores her to intercede with God for us by her prayers.

Blessed Virgin, immaculate and pure, you are the sinless Mother of your Son, who is the mighty Lord of the universe. You are holy and inviolate, the hope of the hopeless and sinful; we sing your praises. We laud you as full of every grace, for you bore the God-Man. We all venerate you; we invoke you and implore your assistance.

Holy and immaculate Virgin, deliver us from every need that weighs upon us and from all the temptations of the devil. Be our intercessor and advocate at the hour of death and judgment. Save us from the fire that is not extinguished and from the outer darkness.

Render us worthy of the glory of your Son, O dearest and most gracious Virgin Mother. You indeed are our most secure and sole hope for you are holy in the sight of God, to whom be honor and glory, majesty and power forever.

4. Mary, Mother of Grace

In this brief prayer, St. Athanasius (d. 373), the champion of Mary's title as Mother of God, addresses her as the one to whom the Son of God granted all graces and begs her to give us the riches of her graces.

It is becoming for you, O Mary, to be mindful of us, as you stand near him who bestowed upon you all graces, for you are the Mother of God and our Queen. Come to our aid for the sake of the King, the Lord God and Master who was born of you. For this reason you are called "full of grace."

Be mindful of us, most holy Virgin, and bestow on us gifts from the riches of your graces, O Virgin full of grace.

5. Mary, Unsurpassed in Dignity

In this simple prayer, St. John Chrysostom upholds Mary's surpassing dignity over Angels and Saints and asks her to pray to her Son for her children on earth so that they may one day attain the things of heaven.

Do you want to know how much our Mother Mary surpasses in dignity the citizens of heaven? Whereas they stand before God with fear and trembling, covering their faces with their wings, she offers up the human race to him to whom she gave birth. It is through her that we may obtain pardon for our sins.

Hail then, O Mother, heavenly being, Virgin-throne of God, glory and bulwark of the Church. Pray for us to Jesus, your Son, our Lord, that through you we may find mercy on the day of judgment and attain to the good things laid up for those who love God.

6. Mary, Mother of Mercy

In this prayer, St. Augustine (d. 430) implicitly anticipates Mary's title "Mother of Mercy," by the emphasis he places on her ability to obtain forgiveness of sins for us.

Blessed Virgin Mary, who can worthily repay you with praise and thanksgiving for rescuing a fallen world by your generous consent? What songs of praise can our weak human nature offer in your honor, since it was through you that it has found the way to salvation?

Accept then such poor thanks as we have to offer, unequal though they be to your merits. Receive our gratitude and obtain by your prayers the forgiveness of our sins. Take our prayers into the sanctuary of heaven and enable them to make our peace with God.

May the sins we repentantly bring before Almighty God through you be forgiven. May what we beg with confidence be granted through you. Accept our offering and grant our request; obtain pardon for what we fear, for you are the sole hope of sinners. We hope to obtain the pardon of our sins through you. Blessed Lady, in you is our hope of reward.

Holy Mary, help those who are miserable, strengthen those who are discouraged, comfort those who are sorrowful, pray for your people, plead for the clergy, intercede for all women consecrated to God. May all who venerate you experience your assistance and protection.

Be ready to aid us when we pray, and bring back to us the answers to our prayers. Make it your continual concern to pray for the People of God, for you were blessed by God and were made worthy to bear the Redeemer of the world, who lives and reigns forever.

7. Mary, Mother of God

In this beautiful prayer, a Father of the Council of Ephesus (431) pays homage to Mary, Mother of God, during the Council itself.

Hail Mary, Mother of God, venerable treasure of the whole world. You are the lamp that is never extinguished, the crown of virginity, the rule of orthodoxy, the incorruptible temple containing the one whom nothing can contain, the Mother and Virgin, through whom the one who comes in the Name of the Lord receives in the Gospel the name of "Blessed."

We salute you, who have borne the immensity of God in your virginal womb. Through you, the Trinity is sanctified. Through you, the Cross is venerated in the whole world. Through you, heaven is filled with joy. Through you, the Angels and Archangels rejoice.

Through you, demons are sent flying. Through you, the tempter devil is cast out of heaven. Through you, the fallen creature is elevated to heaven.

Through you, the whole universe, possessed by idolatry, has attained the knowledge of the truth. Through you, holy Baptism comes to those who believe. Through you, the oil of gladness reaches us.

Through you, churches are established in the whole world. Through you, peoples are led to conversion.

Through you, even more, the only-begotten Son of God has radiated like light upon those who sat in darkness and the shadow of death.

Through you, the Prophets have announced their message, and the Apostles have proclaimed salvation to the nations.

Through you, the dead rise, and kings exercise their royalty, by the power of the Holy Trinity.

8. Mary, Mother and Virgin

In this prayer, St. Cyril of Alexandria (d. 444) enumerates the Mysteries in which Mary was closely involved and sings her praises in phrases that have become common throughout the ages.

Hail, Mother and Virgin, imperishable Temple of the Godhead, venerable treasure of the whole world, crown of virginity, support of the true Faith upon which the Church is founded throughout the whole world.

Mother of God, you enclosed under your heart the infinite God, whom no space can contain. Through you the Most Holy Trinity is revealed, adored and glorified, demons are banished, and our fallen nature is again assumed into heaven. Through you the human race, held captive in the bonds of idolatry, arrives at the knowledge of truth.

Hail, through whom kings rule, through whom the Only-begotten Son of God has become a star of light to those who were sitting in darkness and in the shadow of death!

9. Mary, Blessed above All

In this lyrical prayer, James of Saroug (d. 521) sings Mary's praises in simple and penetrating words that have been used by the Liturgy of the Eastern Church.

Blessed are you, O Mary, and blessed is your holy soul, for your beatitude surpasses that of all the Blessed.

Blessed are you who have borne, embraced, and caressed as a baby the one who upholds the ages with his secret word.

Blessed are you, from whom the Savior appeared on this exile earth, subjugating the seducer and bringing peace to the world.

Blessed are you, whose pure mouth touched the lips of the one whom the Seraphim do not dare to look upon in his splendor.

Blessed are you, who have nourished with your pure milk the source from whom the living obtain life and light.

Blessed are you, because the whole universe resounds with your memory, and the Angels and human beings celebrate your feast....

Daughter of the poor, you became the Mother of the King of kings. You gave to the poor world the riches that can make it live.

You are the bark laden with the goodness and the treasures of the Father, who sent his riches once again into our empty home.

10. Mary, Holier Than the Saints

In this lively prayer, St. Germanus, Bishop of Auxerre (d. 576) extols Mary's holiness, which is higher than any heavenly creature's, by using a host of beautiful images to describe this quality.

Hail Mary, full of grace, more holy than the Saints, more elevated than the heavens, more glorious than the Angels, and more venerable than every creature.

Hail heavenly paradise, all fragrant and a lily that gives off the sweetest scent, a perfumed rose that opens up for the health of mortals.

Hail immaculate temple of the Lord, constructed in a holy fashion, ornament of Divine magnificence, open to everyone, and oasis of mystical delicacies.

Hail mountain of shade, grazing ground for the holy Lamb who takes upon himself the miseries and sins of all.

Hail sacred throne of God, blessed dwelling, sublime ornament, precious jewel, and splendiferous heavens.

Hail urn of purest gold, who contained the manna Christ, the gentle sweetness of our souls.

Hail most pure Virgin Mother, worthy of praise and veneration, fount of gushing waters, treasure of innocence, and splendor of sanctity.

O Mary, lead us to the port of peace and salvation, to the glory of Christ who lives in eternity with the Father and with the Holy Spirit.

11. Mary, Our Leader to True Wisdom

In this very brief prayer, St. Sophronius (d. 640) extols Mary as the Mother of God, foretold by the Prophets, foreshadowed by the Patriarchs, described by the Evangelists, and saluted by the Angels before asking her to lead us to the True Wisdom.

O Mary, Mother of God, you were foretold by the Prophets, foreshadowed by the Patriarchs in types and figures, described by the Evangelists, and saluted most graciously by the Angels. Lead us to the wisdom of the Presence of God now and forever.

12. Mary, Model of Life in the Spirit

In this prayer, St. Ildephonsus of Toledo (d. 677) begs our Lady to receive the grace of living in the Spirit, something of which she was the undisputed model.

I ask and beg you, holy Virgin, that from this Spirit who brought Jesus to birth in you I too may receive Jesus. Let my soul receive him from this Spirit who caused your flesh to conceive him. May I love Jesus in this Spirit in whom you yourself worshiped him as your Lord and contemplated him as your Son.

13. Mary, Life of Christians

In this prayer, St. Germanus of Constantinople (d. 732), one of the greatest Marian Fathers, beautifully portrays our Lady as the very life of Christians.

Who could know God, if it were not for you, most holy Mary? Who could be saved? Who would be preserved from dangers? Who would receive any grace, if it were not for you, Mother of God, full of grace?

What hope could we have of salvation if you were to abandon us, O Mary, who are the life of Christians?

14. Mary, Cause of Our Joy

In this prayer, St. Andrew of Crete (d. 740), another devoted client of Mary, praises her as our greatest intercessor. By her prayers, she has freed us from the sentence of damnation and led us to salvation.

Hail Mary, full of grace, the Lord is with you. I salute you, O

Cause of our Joy, through whom the sentence of our condemnation has been revoked and changed into one of blessings. Hail temple of God's glory, sacred home of the heavenly king! You are God's reconciliation with the human race.

Hail Mother of our joy and gladness! You are indeed blessed, because out of all women you alone have been found worthy to be the Mother of your Creator. All generations call you blessed.

O Mary, if I put my trust in you, I shall be saved; if I am under your protection, I have nothing to fear. For being your servant means possessing salvation, which God grants only to those whom he wills to save.

O Mother of mercy, placate your beloved Son. While on earth, you occupied only a small part of it. However, now that you have been raised above the highest heavens, the whole world regards you as the intercessor of all nations.

We implore you, therefore, O holy Virgin, to grant us the help of your prayers with God, which prayers are dearer to us than all the treasures of the earth. They render God propitious to us in our sins and obtain for us a great abundance of graces, including the grace to receive pardon for our sins and the grace to practice virtue. Your prayers check our enemies, confound their plans, and triumph over their efforts.

15. A Portrait of Mary

In this prayer of praise, St. John Damascene (d. 754), the last Father of the Church in the East, sets forth a beautiful portrait of our Lady replete with Biblical allusions.

Today, the root of Jesse has produced its shoot: she will bring forth a Divine flower for the world.... Today, the Creator of all things, God the Word, composes a new book: a book issuing from the heart of his Father and written by the Holy Spirit, who is the tongue of God....

O daughter of King David and Mother of God, the universal King; O Divine and living object whose beauty has charmed God the Creator; your whole soul is completely open to God's action and attentive to God alone.

All your desires are centered only on what merits to be sought and is worthy of love. You harbor anger only for sin and its author. You will have a life superior to nature — but not for your own sake. For it has not been created for you but has been entirely consecrated to God, who has introduced you into the world to help bring about our salvation in fulfillment of his plan — the Incarnation of his Son and the Divinization of the human race.

Your heart will find nourishment in the words of God, like the tree planted near the living waters of the Spirit, like the tree of life that has yielded its fruit in due time — the incarnate God who is the life of all things.

Your ears will be ever attentive to the Divine words and the sounds of the harp of the Spirit, through whom the Word has come to take on our flesh.... Your nostrils will inhale the fragrance of the Bridegroom, the Divine fragrance with which he scented his humanity.

Your lips will savor the words of God and will rejoice in their Divine sweetness. Your most pure heart, free from all stain, will ever see the God of all purity and will experience ardent desire for him.

Your womb will be the abode of the one whom no place can contain. Your milk will provide nourishment for God, in the little Infant Jesus.... Your hands will carry God, and your knees will serve as a throne for him that is more noble than the throne of the Cherubim....

Your feet, led by the light of the Divine Law, will follow him along an undeviating course and guide you to the possession of the Beloved.

You are the temple of the Holy Spirit, the city of the living God, made joyous by abundant flowers, the sacred flowers of Divine grace. You are all-beautiful and very close to God, above the Cherubim and higher than the Seraphim, right near God himself!

16. Mary, to Whom God Is a Debtor

In this prayer, St. Methodius (d. 847) emphasizes our Lady as the one to whom God is a debtor. She is above all the Saints and is able to intercede for us with her Son.

Your name, O Mother of God, is replete with all graces and Divine blessings. You have contained him who cannot be contained, and nourished him who nourishes all creatures.

He who fills heaven and earth, and is the Lord of all, was pleased to be in need of you, for it was you who clothed him with that flesh which he did not have before. Rejoice, then, O Mother and Handmaid of God!

Rejoice, because you have made him a debtor who gives being to all creatures. We are all debtors to God, but he is a debtor to you.

That is why, O most holy Mother of God, you possess more goodness and greater charity than all the other Saints, and have freer access to God than any of them, for you are his Mother. Be mindful of us, we beg you, in our miseries, for we celebrate your glories and know how great is your goodness.

17. Mary, Our Inviolate Mother

In this little prayer from the eleventh century, the unknown author lauds the purity of our Lady and begs her to help us keep our bodies and souls pure and obtain eternal pardon for us.

O Mary, you are inviolate, pure and without stain, you who became the glistening gate of heaven. O most dear and gracious Mother of Jesus, receive our modest songs of praise.

We beg you with heart and lips: make our bodies and our souls pure. By your sweet prayers, obtain eternal pardon for us. O Mother most kind! O Queen! O Mary! who alone remained inviolate!

18. Mary, Our Advocate

In this prayer, St. Gregory of Narek (d. 1010), the great Doctor of the Armenian Church, calls Mary our Advocate and asks her to obtain the miracle of forgiveness and mercy for those who invoke her.

Assist me by the wings of your prayers, O you who are called the Mother of the living, so that on my exit from this valley of tears I may be able to advance without torment to the dwelling of life that has been prepared for us to lighten the end of a life burdened by my iniquity.

Healer of the sorrows of Eve, change my day of anguish into a feast of gladness. Be my Advocate, ask and supplicate. For as I believe in your inexpressible purity, so do I also believe in the good reception that is given to your word.

O you who are blessed among women, help me with your tears for I am in danger. Bend the knee to obtain my reconciliation, O Mother of God.

Be solicitous for me for I am miserable, O Tabernacle of the Most High. Hold out your hand to me as I fall, O heavenly Temple.

Glorify your Son in you: may he be pleased to operate Divinely in me the miracle of forgiveness and mercy. Handmaid and Mother of God, may your honor be exalted by me, and may my salvation be manifested through you.

19. Mary, Our All-Powerful Ally in Heaven

In this prayer, long attributed to St. Peter Damian (d. 1072), the author calls Mary "omnipotent in heaven and on earth" — but only because the omnipotence comes from her Divine Son — and begs her to obtain forgiveness for all her children on earth.

O holy Virgin, Mother of God, help those who implore your assistance. Turn toward us. Have you perhaps forgotten us because you have been elevated to a position close to God? No, certainly not.

You know well in what danger you left us. You know the miserable condition of your servants. No, it would not benefit such great mercy as yours to forget such great misery as ours.

Turn toward us, then, with your power, for he who is powerful has made you omnipotent in heaven and on earth. For you, nothing is impossible. You can raise even those who are in despair to a hope of salvation. The more powerful you are, the greater should be your mercy.

Turn also to us in your love. I know, O Mary, that you are all kindness and that you love us with a love that no other love can surpass. How often you appease the wrath of our Divine Judge, when he is on the point of punishing us!

All the treasures of the mercy of God are in your hands. You will never cease to benefit us, I know, for you are only seeking an opportunity to save all sinners and to shower your mercies upon them. Your glory is increased when, through you, penitents are forgiven and reach heaven.

Turn, then, toward us, so that we may also be able to go and see you in heaven. For the greatest glory that we can have, after seeing God, will be to see you, to love you, and to be under your protection. So be pleased to grant our prayer; for your beloved Son wishes to honor you by refusing nothing that you ask.

20. The Mother of God Is Our Mother

In this prayer of praise in honor of our Lady, St. Anselm of Canterbury (d. 1086) reminds us that Mary is the Mother of Justification, Reconciliation, and Salvation. Most important of all, because of Mary, Christ is our Brother.

O Blessed Lady, you are the Mother of Justification and of those who are justified; the Mother of Reconciliation and of those who are reconciled; the Mother of Salvation and of those who are saved. What a blessed trust, and what a secure refuge! The Mother of God is our Mother. The Mother of the one in whom alone we hope and whom alone we fear is our Mother!...

The one who partook of our nature and by restoring us to life made us children of his Mother invites us by this to proclaim that we are his brothers and sisters. Therefore, our Judge is also our Brother. The Savior of the world is our Brother. Our God has become — through Mary — our Brother.

21. Mary, Our Mediatrix

In this prayer, one of the greatest Marian Doctors, St. Bernard of Clairvaux (d. 1153), calls upon our Lady as our Mediatrix and Advocate. He asks her to intercede for us with her Son, who came to share our infirmity that we may share his glory.

O blessed Lady, you found grace, brought forth the Life, and became the Mother of salvation. Obtain the grace for us to go to the Son. By your mediation, help us to be received by the one who through you gave himself to us.

May your integrity compensate with him for the fault of our corruption; and may your humility, which is pleasing to God, implore forgiveness for our vanity. May your great charity cover the multitude of our sins; and may your glorious fecundity confer on us a fecundity of merits.

Dear Lady, our Mediatrix and Advocate, reconcile us to your Son, recommend us to him, and lead us to him. By the grace you found, by the privilege you merited, by the Mercy you brought forth, obtain for us the following favor, O blessed Lady.

May the one who, thanks to you, came down to share our infirmity and misery make us share, again thanks to you, his glory and beatitude: Jesus Christ, your Son, our Lord, who reigns in heaven and is blessed forever!

22. Mary, Healer of the Sick

In this prayer, Peter the Venerable (d. 1156) sets forth a number of an-cient titles of Mary and asks her to come to the aid of her suffering clients. Most of all he begs her to remain always alert for their prayers.

Hail, Morning Star, Healer of the sick, Princess and Queen of the world. The only one to be worthy of the name Virgin, you stand up to the blows of the Enemy, and you erect the power of faith like a shield of salvation.

Hail, O root of Jesse, in whom God has begun to exist. Hail, O flowering branch of Aaron, who take away the scandal of the world. Hail, O air moist with rain, totally permeated with the dew of heaven, while the fleece remains dry.

O you who take pity on us, as on prisoners, come to our aid. You are the chosen Spouse of God, full of God's grace. Be for us a right way that leads to joys without end. Preserve an attentive ear for us, O sweet Mary, and hear us always.

23. Mary, Mother of Sacred Healing

In this prayer, St. Hildegard of Bingen (d. 1179) offers strong praise to our Lady as the Mother of sacred healing because of her part in the redemption and asks her to pray to her Son for us.

Radiant Mother of sacred healing, O Mary, you poured salve on the lamentable wounds that Eve caused to torment our souls. For your salve is your Son, and you destroyed death forever, giving rise to life. Pray for us to your Child, O Mary, Star of the Sea.

You are the source of life, sign of gladness, and sweetness of all unfailingly flowing delights. Pray for us to your Child, O Mary, Star of the Sea. Glorify the Father, the Spirit, and the Son. Pray for us to your Child, O Mary, Star of the Sea.

24. Mary, Beloved of the Trinity

In this prayer, St. Francis of Assisi (d. 1226) calls Mary the Daughter of the Father, Mother of the Son, and Spouse of the Holy Spirit, and he venerates her for the graces and virtues she brings into the hearts of her clients.

Holy Virgin Mary, there is none like you among women born in the world. You are the Daughter and Handmaid of the heavenly Father, the Almighty King, Mother of our Most High Lord Jesus Christ, and Spouse of the Holy Spirit. Pray for us to your most holy Son, our Lord and Master.

Hail, holy Lady, most noble Queen, Mother of God, Mary ever Virgin! You were chosen by the heavenly Father, who was pleased to honor you with the presence of his most holy Son and Divine Paraclete. You were blessed with the fullness of grace and goodness.

Hail, Temple of God, his dwelling-place, his masterpiece, and his handmaid. Hail, Mother of God, I venerate you for the holy virtues that, through the grace and light of the Holy Spirit, you bring into the hearts of your clients to transform them from unfaithful Christians into faithful children of God.

25. Mary, Our Queen

In this prayer, St. Anthony of Padua (d. 1231) extols Mary as our Queen and the holy Mother of God and begs her to help us live in such a way as to merit the glory and bliss of heaven.

Mary, our Queen, Holy Mother of God, we beg you to hear our prayer. Make our hearts be filled with Divine grace and resplendent with heavenly wisdom. Render them strong with your might and rich in virtue. Pour down upon us the gift of mercy so that we may obtain the forgiveness of our sins.

Help us to live in such a way as to merit the glory and bliss of heaven. May this be granted us by your Son Jesus Who has exalted you above the Angels, has crowned you as Queen, and has seated you with him forever on his refulgent throne.

26. Mary, Refuge of Sinners

In this prayer, William of Auvergne (d. 1249), Bishop of Paris, appeals for mercy to Mary. For she is known as the Mother of Mercy who brought forth the Fountain of Mercy, our Lord Jesus Christ.

O Mother of God, I appeal to you, and I beg you not to reject me, for all the faithful call you the Mother of Mercy. You are the one whose prayers are always heard because you are so dear to God.

You have never refused to show mercy to anyone. Your kindness and affability have never turned away any sinner who recommended himself to you, no matter how great his crimes were. Is the Church wrong or misled when she calls you the Advocate and Mediatrix of peace?

May my sins never be responsible for preventing you from fulfilling your great office of mercy. You are the Advocate and Mediatrix of peace, the only hope and refuge of the miserable. Never let it be said that the Mother of God, who for the benefit of the whole world gave birth to the Fountain of Mercy, should ever refuse mercy to any sinner who turns to her.

Your office is that of a peacemaker between God and human beings. Let, then, the greatness of your compassion, which is far greater than my sins, come to my assistance.

27. Dedication to Mary

In this short prayer, the great Doctor St. Thomas Aquinas (d. 1274) dedicates himself to our Lady with heart and soul and asks that he may always love Jesus and her above all things.

Virgin full of goodness, Mother of mercy, I entrust to you my body and soul, my thoughts and actions, my life and death.

O my Queen, help me, and deliver me from all the snares of the devil. Obtain for me the grace of loving my Lord Jesus Christ, your Son, with a true and perfect love, and, after him, O Mary, to love you with all my heart and above all things.

28. Mary, Ladder to Heaven

In this very brief prayer, St. Bonaventure (d. 1274), one of our Lady's greatest devotees who has written beautiful lengthy Marian prayers, calls her the Ladder to heaven and asks her to assure our pardon and eternal rest.

Holy Virgin, I beg of you, when my soul shall depart from my body, be pleased to meet and receive it.

Mary, do not refuse me then the grace of being sustained by your sweet presence. Be for me the ladder and the way to heaven, and finally assure me of pardon and eternal rest.

29. Mary, Recipient of God's Favor

In this prayer, St. Albert the Great (d. 1280) speaks of our Lady as some-one who has found God's favor because she sought it in the right way. He acclaims her for in doing so she has found Uncreated Grace — Jesus Christ.

"Do not fear, Mary, you have found favor with God" (Luke 1:30). Fear not, Mary, for you have found, not taken grace, as Luci-fer tried to take it. You have not lost it, as Adam lost it.

You have found favor with God because you have desired and sought it. You have found uncreated Grace: that is, God himself became your Son, and with that Grace you have found and obtained every uncreated good.

30. *"Daughter of Your Son"*

In this beautiful prayer from the masterpiece of the Divine Comedy, the poet Dante Alighieri (d. 1321) sings the praises of our Lady as the Daughter of her Son! He does so by placing the prayer on the lips of St. Bernard of Clairvaux.

> O Virgin Mother, daughter of your Son,
> humble and exalted beyond every creature,
> and established term of God's eternal plan,
> you are the one who ennobled human nature
> to such an extent that its Divine Maker
> did not disdain to become its workmanship....
> O Lady, you are so great and powerful
> that those who seek grace without recourse to you
> are expecting wishes to fly without wings.
> Your loving kindness not only comes to the aid
> of those who ask for it
> but very often spontaneously precedes the request for it.
> In you is mercy, in you is pity,
> in you is magnificence, in you is found everything
> that is good in God's creation.

31. *Petition to Mary*

In this prayer, St. Gertrude (d. 1334) calls upon our Lady in her chastity, humility, and charity to obtain cleansing of all stain, pardon of all sins, and an abundance of all merits.

Most chaste Virgin Mary, I beg of you, by that unspotted purity with which you prepared for the Son of God a dwelling of delight in your virginal womb, that by your intercession I may be cleansed from every stain.

Most humble Virgin Mary, I beg of you, by that most profound humility by which you deserved to be raised high above all the choirs of Angels and Saints, that by your intercession all my sins may be expiated.

Most amiable Virgin Mary, I beg of you, by that indescribable love which united you so closely and inseparably to God, that by your intercession I may obtain an abundance of all merits.

32. In Praise of Mary

In this lengthy prayer, St. Catherine of Siena (d. 1380) praises our Lady in words filled with admirable doctrine, filial tenderness toward the Mother of God, and poetry embellished by new and sensitive expressions.

O Mary, Mary, temple of the Trinity. O Mary, bearer of fire. O Mary, dispenser of mercy. O Mary, restorer of human generation, because the world was repurchased by means of the sustenance that your flesh found in the Word. Christ repurchased the world with his Passion, and you with your suffering of mind and body.

O Mary, peaceful ocean. O Mary, giver of peace. O Mary, fruitful land. You, O Mary, are that new plant from which we have the fragrant flower of the Word, only-begotten Son of God, because this Word was sown in you, O fruitful land. You are the land and the plant.

O Mary, vehicle of fire, you bore the fire hidden and veiled beneath the ash of your humanity. O Mary, vase of humility, in which there burns the light of true knowledge with which you lifted yourself above yourself and yet were pleasing to the eternal Father; hence he took and brought you to himself, loving you with a singular love.

With this light and fire of your charity and with the oil of your humility, you inclined his Divinity to come into you — although he was first drawn to come to us by the most ardent fire of his inestimable charity....

Today I ardently make my request, because it is the day of graces, and I know that nothing is refused to you, O Mary. Today, O Mary, your land has generated the Savior for us. O Mary, blessed are you among women throughout the ages!

33. Mary, Worthy of Unending Praises

In this brief prayer, St. Bernardine of Siena (d. 1444) sings a kind of ballad to Mary who is worthy of receiving unending praises from her children. For she is the Mother of God and Queen of the Universe.

O Woman, filled with the blessings of all creatures, you are the sole Mother of God. You are the Queen of the Universe. You are the Dispenser of all graces.

You are the ornament of the Church. In you is contained the ineffable greatness of all virtue and all gifts.

You are the Temple of God, the Paradise of delight, the Model of all the righteous, the Consolation of your children, and the Glory and Source of our salvation.

You are the Gate of heaven, the Joy of the elect, and the Object of God's great plan for his holy People.

Although we celebrate your praises in merely an imperfect way, your love for us makes up for all our deficiencies. May we worthily laud you, our Mother in God, for all eternity.

34. Mary's Right to be Venerated

In this prayer, Thomas à Kempis (d. 1471) sets forth the reasons why our Lady deserves to be venerated. Then he begs Mary to protect us against all evils by her merits and prayers.

O Virgin Mary, we are greatly obliged to venerate you. For you are at the same time Mother and Daughter of the eternal King; you deserve to be blessed by every voice, and you are worthy to receive the greatest honors.

You are the most pure in your virginity, the most profound in your humility, the most fervent in your charity, and the most mild in your patience.

You are the most rich in your mercy, the most ardent in your prayer, the most lucid in your meditation, and the most elevated in your contemplation.

You are the most sensitive in your compassion, the most close in your union with your Son, the most powerful by your aid..., you are the Health of the sick and the Mother of orphans.

You offer us eternal rewards.... Hence, we take refuge in you, like little children in the arms of their mother. Protect us against all evils by your merits and prayers.

35. Our Lady of Virtues

In this prayer, St. Joan of Valois (d. 1505), who founded the Congrega-tion of Nuns of the Annunciation, praises the virtues of Mary, especially those of truthfulness, patience, and charity. She then asks our Lady to help us in our needs.

O Virgin most truthful, the soil from which — in the words of David — Truth sprang forth, grant us the grace to keep in all things truth of heart, of word, and of deed.

O Virgin most patient, grant us patience amid the plenitude of trials and sorrows in this world. In this way, after the storm of adversities, afflictions, and anguish, which assail us on all sides, we may joyfully reach the land of the living, the haven of eternal beati-tude, and there enjoy the everlasting rest prepared for the elect.

O Virgin most charitable, fill our hearts with charity, with love, and with the grace of God. Mother of Mercy — under which title the Church invokes you — have pity on us who are weighed down beneath the burden of our sins and afflictions.

Look upon us, in your Motherly pity, so that your mercy may move you to assist us in our necessities.

36. Self-Commendation to Mary

In this prayer, St. Aloysius Gonzaga (d. 1591) entrusts himself completely and wholeheartedly to our Lady and asks that every action of his be according to her will and that of her Divine Son.

O holy Mary, my Lady, into your blessed trust and safe keeping and into the depths of your mercy I commend my soul and body this day, every day of my life, and at the hour of my death. To you I entrust all my hopes and consolations, all my trials and miseries, my life and the end of my life.

By your most holy intercession and by your merits, may all my actions be directed and disposed according to your will and the Will of your Divine Son.

37. Self-Offering to Mary

In this prayer, St. Francis de Sales (d. 1622) also enlists in the "servant type" of Marian spirituality, promising to commit all of himself to be the servant of Mary his Queen, Advocate, and Mother.

Most holy Mary, virgin Mother of God, most unworthy though I am to be your servant, yet moved by your Motherly care for me and longing to serve you, I choose you this day to be my Queen, my Advocate, and my Mother. I firmly resolve ever to be devoted to you and to do what I can to encourage others to be devoted to you.

My loving Mother, through the Precious Blood of your Son shed for me, I beg you to receive me as your servant forever. Aid me in my actions and beg for me the grace never by word or deed or thought to be displeasing in your sight and that of your most holy Son. Remember me, dearest Mother, and do not abandon me at the hour of death.

38. Prayer of a Slave of Mary

In this prayer, the Augustinian friar Bartolomeo de los Rios (d. 1652) anticipates the "slave of Mary" type of spirituality made popular later by another devoted client, St. Louis de Montfort.

Virgin of virgins, I choose you today as my Sovereign, my Queen, my Empress, and I declare myself — what I really am — your servant and your slave. I invoke your royal name of Mary, namely, sovereign Lady, and beg you with all my heart to take me into the privileged circle of your family as one of your servants, to carry out your will as a humble slave and loving child.

As a sign of your acceptance, let the fire of your love stamp on my heart those two gracious words of the Angel: "Hail Mary" in place of the brand of an unwilling slave. So long as I draw breath, may your ardent love ensure that I will bear these words in my heart and in my memory, and that unto my dying breath my will may be always inflamed with my great desire to serve you, my Sovereign and my Queen, glorious in your majesty.

Although I am completely unworthy of such an honorable title, I sincerely resolve to be your slave, to serve you wholeheartedly, to defend your name and that of your Son from every insult insofar as I can, and never to allow anyone in my care to offend your Son in any way.

By your tender love for your Son and by the glories you have received from the Most Holy Trinity, do not reject me from your service, but as my Sovereign and my Queen preside over all my actions, command anything you will, direct all my work, and remedy all its defects.

Throughout my whole life, rule over me as your servant and slave. At the hour of my death, in keeping with my hope for my loving servitude as one of the privileged members of your family, receive my soul and accompany it into the presence of God.

39. A Litany of Praise to Mary

In this litany-like prayer, St. John Eudes (d. 1640) weaves together a list of Mary's brightest titles and fashions them into a unified whole. He thus gives us a paean of praise to our Lady.

Hail Mary, Daughter of God the Father. Hail Mary, Mother of God the Son. Hail Mary, Spouse of God the Holy Spirit. Hail Mary, Temple of the Most Blessed Trinity. Hail Mary, Pure Lily of the Effulgent Trinity.

Hail Mary, Celestial Rose of the ineffable Love of God. Hail Mary, pure and humble Virgin, of whom the King of Heaven willed to be born and to be nourished by your milk.

Hail Mary, Virgin of virgins. Hail Mary, Queen of martyrs, whose soul was pierced by a sword. Hail Mary, Lady most blessed, to whom is given all power in heaven and on earth.

Hail Mary, my Queen and my Mother, my life, my sweetness, and my hope. Hail Mary, Mother most amiable. Hail Mary, Mother most admirable. Hail Mary, Mother of Divine Love.

Hail Mary, Immaculate, conceived without sin. Hail Mary, full of grace, the Lord is with you. Blessed are you among women, and blessed is the fruit of your womb, Jesus.

Blessed be your Spouse, St. Joseph. Blessed be your father, St. Joachim. Blessed be your mother, St. Ann. Blessed be your guardian, St. John. Blessed be your holy Angel, St. Gabriel.

Glory be to God the Father, who chose you. Glory be to God the Son, who loved you. Glory be to God the Holy Spirit, who espoused you.

O glorious Virgin Mary, may all people love and praise you. Mary, Mother of God, pray for us and bless us, now and at the hour of our death in the Name of Jesus, your Divine Son.

40. The Spirit of Mary

In this prayer, St. Louis de Montfort (d. 1716) asks our Lady to bestow on him her spirit. In doing so he introduces the famous phrase "Totus Tuus"— "All Yours," which is the motto of Pope John Paul II and has become familiar to modern Catholics through him.

Hail Mary, beloved Daughter of the eternal Father. Hail Mary, wonderful Mother of the Son. Hail Mary, faithful Spouse of the Holy Spirit. Hail Mary, my dear Mother, my loving Lady, my powerful Queen. You are all mine through your mercy, and I am all yours. Take away from me all that may be displeasing to God. Cultivate in me everything that is pleasing to you.

May the light of your faith dispel the darkness of my mind; your deep humility take the place of my pride; your continual sight of God fill my memory with his presence; the fire of the charity of your heart inflame the lukewarmness of my own heart; your virtues take the place of my sins; your merits be my enrichment and make up for all that is wanting in me before God.

My beloved Mother, grant that I may have no other spirit but your spirit, to know Jesus Christ and his Divine Will and to praise and glorify the Lord; that I may love God with burning love like yours.

41. Mary, Gentlest of All God's Creatures

In this prayer, Alexander de Rouville, a Jesuit priest who had to write anonymously at the time of the suppression of the Jesuits, praises our Lady's gentleness and asks her help in being good to others. The prayer is found in his outstanding work, The Imitation of Mary.

Virgin, gentlest of all God's creatures, show me how you acted toward the many ungrateful people whom Jesus taught and for whom he worked great miracles. Thus I shall learn how to put up with the faults of my neighbor.

How often you witnessed the ingratitude and betrayal Jesus received in return for the good he did! Yet your thoughts and feelings toward his enemies were like his, only thoughts and feelings of peace.

You detested sin, but you loved the sinner. It was only the offense against God that moved you deeply; you let no complaint against these foolish people pass your lips, and you even took up their cause with Jesus.

You acted toward them as you now act, after so many years, toward me. I am the most faithless and ungrateful of your servants, yet you treat me with kindness and win ever new favors from God for me.

Mother of the God of peace, win for me the grace never again to distress anyone with unkind words. Your very name and image causes me to think mild thoughts. Obtain for me the virtue of gentleness and the spirit of peace, so that I may merit the glorious title of "child of God."

42. Mary, Hope for Salvation

In this prayer, St. Alphonsus Liguori (d. 1787), one of the outstanding Marian Doctors, places his hope for salvation completely in the hands of our Lady and begs her to bring him safely to his heavenly home.

Most holy and immaculate Virgin, my Mother, you are the Mother of my Lord, the Queen of the world, the advocate, hope, and refuge of sinners. I, the most miserable among them, come to you today. I venerate you, great Queen, and thank you for the many graces you have bestowed on me. I thank you especially for having saved me so many times from the punishment of God that I deserved.

I love you, most lovable Lady. By the love that I have for you, I promise ever to serve you, and to do as much as I can to make you loved by others.

I put all my hope in you, my entire salvation. Receive me as your servant, Mother of mercy, and cover me with the mantle of your protection. Since you are so powerful with God, free me from all temptations, or, at least, obtain for me the grace to overcome them until death.

I ask of you a true love for Jesus Christ. Through you I hope to die a good death. My Mother, by the love you have for God, I beg you to help me always, and most of all at the last moment of my life. Do not leave me until you see me safe in heaven. I hope to thank and praise you there forever.

43. Consecration of the United States to Mary

In this prayer, John Carroll (d. 1815), the first Archbishop of the United States, consecrated his new country to Mary. He begs God to safeguard the young nation because of the gracious protection of our Lady.

Most Holy Trinity, our Father in heaven, who chose Mary as the fairest of your daughters; Holy Spirit, who chose Mary as your Spouse; God the Son, who chose Mary as your Mother; in union with Mary, we adore your Majesty and acknowledge your supreme, eternal dominion and authority.

Most Holy Trinity, we place the United States of America into the hands of Mary Immaculate in order that she may present the country to you. Through her we wish to thank you for the great resources of this land and for the freedom which has been its heritage.

Through the intercession of Mary, have mercy on the Catholic Church in America. Grant us peace. Have mercy on our President and on all the officers of our government.

Grant us a fruitful economy, born of justice and labor. Protect the family life of the nation. Guard the precious gift of many religious vocations. Through the intercession of Mary our Mother, have mercy on the sick, the tempted, sinners... on all who are in need.

Mary, Immaculate Virgin, our Mother, Patroness of our land, we praise and honor you and give ourselves to you. Protect us from every harm. Pray for us, that acting always according to your will and the will of your Divine Son, we may live and die pleasing to God.

44. Our Lady of the Suffering

In this prayer, Abbe Henri Perreyve (d. 1865) addresses our Lady on her throne of glory and asks her not to forget those who are still struggling heavenward on their earthly pilgrimage, but to give them the hope of peace.

O Holy Virgin, in the midst of your days of glory do not forget the sorrows of earth. Cast a kindly glance upon those who are suffering, those who struggle against difficulties and maintain a stiff upper lip in all life's afflictions.

Have mercy on those who love one another and have been separated.

Have mercy on those who suffer from isolation of the heart.

Have mercy on the weakness of our faith.

Have mercy on those we love.

Have mercy on those who pray, those who tremble, and those who weep.

Give to all the hope of peace.

45. Mary, Our Queen Enthroned on High

In this prayer, St. Catherine Labouré (d. 1876) praises Mary as our Queen enthroned in heaven who is both the Mother of God and our Mother. She then asks our Lady to obtain our welfare and that of the whole world.

O Queen full of goodness, from the sublime throne on which you are seated next to Jesus Christ, be pleased to receive the pleas of those who implore your help.

Mother of God, you have the power to move your Son. You are also our Mother, and you love us as your children. May you who have access to the very source of graces pour down on us grace in abundance.

Present our pleas and our prayers to God. He will scarcely refuse anything to a Mother that he loves so much!...

O Mary, your name is our defense; protect us. O Mary, you are the refuge of sinners and our Mother....

O Mary, see the danger in which we find ourselves, and have mercy on us. Do not hesitate to listen to our pleas. If you but deign to implore your Son, he will hear you. If you are willing to save us, we will not lack for being saved....

O Mary, tell us what to ask from you for our welfare, so that it will overflow into the benefit of the entire world.

46. Mary, Our Model in Suffering

In this prayer, St. Bernadette (d. 1879), the young visionary who saw the Immaculate Conception and initiated the shrine that ultimately became Lourdes, begs our Lady to bear her own sufferings as she, the Mother of God, did in her lifetime and so merit a heart burning with love for Jesus.

O Mary, you became my Mother at the height of suffering and trials. Hence, I must have a great and complete trust in you. Whenever I undergo trials at the hands of creatures and experience temptation and desolation of soul, let me take refuge in your Heart, my Good Mother, and call upon you for help.

Do not let me perish but grant me the grace to be patient and confident in trials after your example. Let me suffer with love. Let me stand, like you, at the foot of the Cross, if that is the Will of your dear Son.

Never will anyone perish who is a devoted child of Mary. O good Mother, have mercy on me. I give myself entirely to you so that you may present me to your dear Son, whom I want to love with all my heart. Confer on me, good Mother, a heart burning with love for Jesus.

47. Mary, Help of Christians

In this prayer, St. John Bosco (d. 1888) stresses the great power of our Lady to come to the aid of Christians in their material as well as spiritual adversities, and he asks her to help us at the most important hour of our death.

Mary, powerful Virgin, you are the mighty and glorious protector of the Church. You are the marvelous help of Christians. You are awe-inspiring as an army set in battle array. You have eliminated heresy in the world.

In the midst of our anguish, our struggle, and our distress, defend us from the power of the enemy, and at the hour of our death receive our soul in heaven.

48. Mary, Our Guide to Heaven

In this prayer, St. Thérèse of the Child Jesus (d. 1897) applies her "Little Way" to the life of our Lady as shown in the Gospel. She asks Mary to guide all "the little ones" to heaven.

Virgin full of grace, I know that at Nazareth you lived modestly, without requesting anything more. Neither ecstasies, nor miracles, nor other extraordinary deeds embellished your life, O Queen of the Elect.

The number of the lowly, "the little ones," is very great on earth. They can lift their eyes to you without any fear.

You are the incomparable Mother who walks by their side along the common way in order to guide them to heaven. Beloved Mother, in this difficult exile, I want to live always with you and follow you day after day. I am captivated by the contemplation of you and I discover the depths of the love of your Heart. All my fears vanish under your Motherly gaze, which teaches me to weep and to rejoice!

49. Our Lady of the Sacred Heart

In this prayer, attributed to an unknown hand of the nineteenth-twentieth century, the author addresses Mary as Our Lady of the Sacred Heart and asks her to enable us to live, as she did, in the love of her Son so that his Kingdom may come.

Our Lady of the Sacred Heart, remember all the wonders that the Lord accomplished for you. He chose you for his Mother and willed you to stand by the Cross. He made you share his glory, and he listens to your prayer.

Offer him our praises and our gratitude, and place our requests before him. Enable us to live, as you did, in the love of your Son, so that his Kingdom may come.

Lead all human beings to the source of living water, which springs forth from his Heart, filling the whole world with hope and salvation, justice and peace.

See our confidence, respond to our call, and show yourself to be ever our Mother.

50. Mary, Our Refuge

In this prayer, the great "Pope of the Rosary," Leo XIII (d. 1903) holds our Lady up as the refuge of her clients and begs her to let them find rest in her Motherly embrace.

It is sweet music to the ear to say: I salute you, O Mother! It is a sweet song to repeat: I salute you, O Mother! You are my delight, dear hope, and chaste love.

If my spirit that is troubled and stricken by passions suffers from the painful burden of sadness and weeping; if you see your child overwhelmed by misfortune, O gracious Virgin Mary, let me find rest in your Motherly embrace.

But alas, already the last day is quickly approaching. Banish the demon to the infernal depths, and stay close, dear Mother, to your aged and erring child. With a gentle touch, cover the weary pupils and kindly consign to God the soul that is returning to you.

51. Our Lady of the Trinity

In this prayer, Bl. Elizabeth of the Trinity (d. 1906) focuses on our Lady's relation to the Persons of the Blessed Trinity and asks Mary to guard her in a perpetual Divine embrace and impress on her the imprint of the God of love.

O faithful Virgin, night and day you remain in a profound silence, in an ineffable peace, and in a Divine prayer that never ceases, with your soul completely inundated by eternal splendors. Your heart reflects, like crystal, the Divine.

O Mary, you attract heaven, and behold the Father entrusts to you his Word so that you may be his Mother, and the Spirit of love covers you with his shadow. The Three Persons come to you, and the whole of heaven opens up to you and lowers itself to you. I worship the Mystery of this God who becomes incarnate in you, O Virgin Mother.

O Mother of the Word, tell me your mystery after the Incarnation of the Lord: how you spent your time on earth all suffused with adoration. Guard me forever in a Divine embrace, that I may carry within me the imprint of this God of love.

52. Our Lady of Hearts

In this prayer, Father Leonce de Grandmaison (d. 1927), theologian and apologist, follows the little way of St. Thérèse of the Child Jesus and asks our Lady for the gift of a simple heart.

Holy Mary, Mother of God, preserve in me the heart of a child, pure and simple like water from a fount.

Obtain for me a simple heart that does not savor distresses; a magnanimous heart in giving itself and quick to show compassion; a faithful and generous heart that does not forget any good and holds no rancor for any evil.

Fashion for me a kind and humble heart that loves and does not look for any return, joyous to be effaced in another heart, before your Divine Son; a large and indomitable heart that no ingratitude can cause to close and no indifference can weary; a heart driven by the glory of Jesus Christ and wounded by his love with a gash that can be healed only in heaven.

53. Consecration to Our Lady

In this prayer, St. Maximilian Kolbe (d. 1941), one of the greatest Marian Doctors, who offered his life for another in a concentration camp during the Second World War, makes a total commitment to Mary and asks for her help in keeping it.

Immaculate Virgin, grant that I may sing your praise with my total commitment and my personal sacrifice. Grant that I may live, work, suffer, be consumed, and give my life for you.

May I contribute to an ever greater exaltation of you and render more glory to you than anyone has ever done in the past.

Grant that others may surpass me in zeal for your exaltation and that I may in turn surpass them. Thus, in a noble emulation, your glory may ever increase, in accord with the desire of the one who exalted you above all creatures.

God is more glorified in you than in all his Saints. Through you God has created the world, and through you he has called me into existence.

Make me worthy to praise you, O Immaculate Virgin.

54. A Silent Contemplation of Mary

In this prayer, the world-famous poet and dramatist Paul Claudel (d. 1955) offers a touching song of the heart to our Lady out of his overflowing love for her. He asks nothing of Mary except to sit quietly in the presence of her who has given the world its Divine Savior.

It is noon. I see the church open, and I must enter. Mother of Jesus Christ, I do not come to pray. I have nothing to offer and nothing to request.

I come solely to gaze on you, O Mother. To gaze on you, to weep for joy, and to know this: that I am your child and you are there.

I come only for a moment while everything is at a standstill, at noon!

Just be with me, O Mary, in this place where you are. Not to say anything but to gaze at your countenance, and let the heart sing in its own language; not to say anything but solely to sing because my heart is overflowing.

For you are beautiful, because you are immaculate, the woman fully restored in Grace, the creature in its pristine honor and its final bloom, as it issued from God on the morn of its original splendor.

You are ineffably intact, because you are the Mother of Jesus Christ, who is the Truth in your arms, and the only hope and the sole fruit.

55. Mary, Our Strength

In this prayer, Pope Pius XII (d. 1958), the Pope who solemnly declared the dogma of the Assumption, presents our Lady as the strength of Christians and asks for her help in our pilgrimage through life.

O Virgin, fair as the moon, delight of the Angels and Saints in heaven, grant that we may become like you and that our souls may receive a ray of your beauty, which does not decline with the years but shines forth into eternity.

O Mary, sun of heaven, restore life where there is darkness. Turn your countenance to your children and radiate on us your light and your fervor.

O Mary, powerful as an army, grant victory to our ranks. We are very weak and our enemy rages with uttermost conceit. But under your banner we are confident of overcoming him....

Save us, O Mary, fair as the moon, bright as the sun, awe-inspiring as an army set in battle array and sustained not by hatred but by the ardor of love.

56. Recourse to Mary

In this prayer, Pope John XXIII (d. 1963), the Pope who called the Second Vatican Council, testifies to his love for our Lady and asks for her help in his earthly vocation.

O Mary, your Name is always on my lips and in my heart. From infancy I learned to love you as my Mother, to call upon you in dangers, and to trust in your intercession. You know my desire to seek truth and do good....

O Mary, sustain me in my will to live as a faithful disciple of Jesus so as to build up Christian society and gladden the holy Catholic Church.

Dear Mother, I greet you morning and night; I invoke you along the way; and from you I await the inspiration and consolation to crown the holy tasks of my earthly vocation, give glory to God, and obtain eternal salvation.

O Mary, in imitation of you at Bethlehem and on Calvary, I too wish to remain always close to Jesus, the immortal King of ages and of peoples.

57. Mary, Mother of the Church

In this prayer, Pope Paul VI (d. 1978), the Pope who saw the completion of Vatican II and helped insert the section on Marian doctrine in the Constitution on the Church, *prays to Mary under the title "Mother of the Church," a title that he was instrumental in giving her.*

O Mary, look upon the Church, look upon the most responsible members of the Mystical Body of Christ gathered about you to thank you and to celebrate you as their Mystical Mother.

O Mary, bless the great assembly of the hierarchical Church, which also gives birth to brothers and sisters of Christ, the firstborn among redeemed humankind.

O Mary, grant that this Church of Christ — in defining herself — will acknowledge you as her most chosen Mother, Daughter, and Sister as well as her incomparable model, her glory, her joy, and her hope.

We ask you now that we may be made worthy of honoring you because of who you are and because of what you do in the wondrous and loving plan of salvation. Grant that we may praise you, O holy Virgin!....

O Mary, look upon all humankind, this modern world in which the Divine Will calls us to live and work: It is a world that has turned its back on the light of Christ; then it fears and bemoans the frightening shadows that its actions have created on all sides.

May your most human voice, O most beautiful of virgins, O most worthy of mothers, O blessed among woman, invite the world to turn its eyes toward the life that is the light of human beings, toward you who are the precursor-lamp of Christ, who is the sole and the highest Light of the world.

Implore for the world the true understanding of its own existence; implore for the world the joy of living as the creation of God and hence the desire and the capacity to converse — by prayer — with its Maker, whose mysterious and blessed image it reflects within itself.

Implore for the world the grace to esteem everything as a gift of God and hence the virtue to work with generosity and to make use of such gifts wisely and providentially.

Implore peace for the world. Fashion brothers and sisters out of persons who are so divided. Guide us to a more ordered and peaceful society.

For those who are suffering — today there are so many and ever new ones, afflicted by current misfortunes — obtain solace; and for the dead, obtain eternal rest.

Show yourself a Mother to us: this is our prayer, O clement, O loving, O sweet Virgin Mary!

58. Mary, Mother of All

In this prayer, Pope John Paul II, a Pope so devoted to our Lady that his Marian motto is "All Yours" and who by his strong devotion to the Mother of God has effected a new springtime in devotion to her, prays to Mary for the entire human family as we approach the Third Millennium.

Mother of the Redeemer... with great joy we call you blessed.

In order to carry out his providential plan of salvation, God the Father chose you before the creation of the world. You believed in his love and obeyed his word.

The Son of God desired you for his Mother when he became man to save the human race. You received him with ready obedience and undivided heart. The Holy Spirit loved you as his mystical Spouse and he filled you with singular gifts. You allowed yourself to be led by his hidden and powerful action.

On the eve of the Third Christian Millennium, we entrust to you the Church, which acknowledges you and invokes you as Mother. On earth you preceded the Church in the pilgrimage of faith: comfort her in her difficulties and trials, and make her always the sign and instrument of intimate union with God and of the unity of the whole human race....

To you, Mother of the human family and of the nations, we confidently entrust the whole of humanity, with its hopes and fears. Do not let it lack the light of true wisdom. Guide its steps in the ways of peace. Enable all to meet Christ, the Way and the Truth and the Life.

Sustain us, O Virgin Mary, on our journey of faith and obtain for us the grace of eternal salvation. O clement, O loving, O sweet Mother of God and our Mother, Mary!

59. Consecration to Our Lady of Fatima

Through this prayer, attributed to an unknown hand in our day, faithful clients of our Lady can consecrate all that they are and all that they have to Our Lady of Fatima and ask for the coming of Christ's Kingdom.

O Virgin of Fatima, Mother of Mercy, Queen of Heaven and Earth, Refuge of Sinners, we consecrate ourselves to your Immaculate Heart in order to enter into a more intimate relationship with your Divine Son, Jesus Christ. To you we consecrate our hearts, our families, and all that we have.

So that this consecration may be effective and lasting, we renew today, and every day, the promises of our Baptism: we promise to live as faithful Christians, to read the Sacred Scriptures, to pray, especially the Rosary of your Son, to partake of the Holy Eucharist, to observe the First Saturdays of Reparation each month, and to work and sacrifice for the conversion of sinners, especially ourselves.

We pray that through your intercession the coming of the Kingdom of Christ may be hastened.

60. Consecration to Our Lady of Guadalupe

Through this prayer, attributed to an unknown hand in our day, faithful clients of our Lady can consecrate all that they are and all that they have to Our Lady of Guadalupe and promise to live a life of reparation to her Immaculate Heart.

O most holy Virgin Mary, Mother of God, I (N.), although most unworthy of being your servant, yet touched by your wonderful mercy and by the desire to serve, consecrate myself to your Immaculate Heart, and choose you today, in the presence of my Guardian Angel and the whole heavenly court, for my special Mother, Lady, and Advocate, under the title of Our Lady of Guadalupe, the name given to the heavenly image left to us as a pledge of your Motherly goodness.

I firmly resolve that I will love and serve you. I pray to you, Mother of God, and my most kind and amiable Mother, that you receive me into your family and keep me as your special child forever.

Assist me in all my thoughts, words, and actions at every moment of my life, that every step and breath may be directed to the greater glory of God; and through your most powerful intercession, obtain for me that I may never more offend my Lord Jesus, that I may glorify him in this life, and that I may also love you and be with you, in the company of the Blessed Trinity throughout eternity in holy Paradise.

In order to live this consecration as did Juan Diego, I promise to renew it frequently, especially on the twelfth day of each month; and mindful of your messages to us at Lourdes and Fatima and Akita, I will strive to lead a life of prayer and sacrifice, of fidelity to the Rosary and of reparation to your Immaculate Heart.

This book was designed and published by St. Pauls/
Alba House, the publishing arm of the Society of St.
Paul, an international religious congregation of
priests and brothers dedicated to serving the Church
through the communications media. For information
regarding this and associated ministries of the
Pauline Family of Congregations, write to the Vocation Director, Society of St. Paul, 7050 Pinehurst,
Dearborn, Michigan 48126 or check our internet site,
www.albahouse.org